Changing Society

A personal history of Scope
(formerly The Spastics Society)
1952–2002

by

Chris Davies

with a foreword by Jonathan Dimbleby

1952-2002
FIFTY YEARS

The Mirror

In 1952, over 300 readers responded to a letter in the 'Daily Mirror' that helped form The National Spastics Society, the national disability organisation now known as Scope. The paper went on to publish a series of cartoons about the experience of having a child with cerebral palsy in the family, which are reproduced in this book with its kind permission.

In 2002, as Scope celebrates its 50th Anniversary, we would like to thank 'The Mirror' for its kind support in paying for the printing of this history in recognition of this special relationship.

Acknowledgements

Where do I start? Do I begin with those who have helped me professionally or do I first mention those who have been personally supportive?

If I begin with the personal 'credits', there's only one place to start. My Mum, who believed in me all these years and who pushed and shoved me into being who I am now. Next are all my Personal Assistants who were my arms and legs through the process of writing this book. All the interviews were recorded on Mini Disc, which, thanks to Rob Perks of the National Sound Archive, can be heard at the British Library accession number C984 – visit www.cadensa.bl.uk to access the collection. My technician who pressed the button on the recorder was Chris Baldwin. Other personal assistants involved doing the dictation have been Di Carroll, Lucy Reed, Simon (Charlie) Lee, Tim Butler, Georgina Aldous and Scott Smith.

Professionally, my thanks go to James Rye, who commissioned my idea; Alex White, who co-ordinated the book and did the picture research; Bill Elliott, who did much of the historical research; and Patrick Bond, who proofread the book. Without the support of James and Alex, this book would not exist. Without the information provided by Bill Elliott I would have probably been lost.

But, of course, this book would be nothing without the people I interviewed. My sincere thanks to them for their co-operation and support.

Finally, what would Scope be without the people who support it? Anyone who ever benefits from Scope owes a lot to the members of the public who choose to back the organisation. The first 50 years would not have happened without your support, I trust it will go on for another 50 years.

Every effort has been made to credit the photographers in this book. We would like to thank the photographers we were able to contact for their permission to reproduce their work.

© Scope 2002

ISBN 0946828962

Produced by Scope Creative Services (CS3069)

Printed by Antony Rowe, Chippenham, Wiltshire

Copies obtainable from:

Library and Information Unit,
Scope, 6 Market Road, London N7 9PW

Credit card orders 020 7619 7341

Contents

Foreword by Jonathan Dimbleby	1
Introductions	5
Fifties, Beginnings	15
Sixties, Expansion	45
Seventies, Being There	63
Eighties, Evaluation and Rebirth	85
Nineties, Changing for the 21st Century	113
2000 and Beyond	143
Conclusions	165

Changing Society

Foreword

by Jonathan Dimbleby

In 1964, my father, Richard Dimbleby, the most eminent broadcaster in Britain and a passionate advocate for disabled people, helped put together *Every Eight Hours*, the first-ever history of The Spastics Society (now known as Scope). This was a landmark year for the charity, which had completed its merger with the British Council for the Welfare of Spastics in the previous year and was looking to the future.

I know that my father was full of admiration for the energy and drive of the Society's founders, Ian Dawson-Shepherd, Eric Hodgson, Jean Garwood and Alex Moira. They met in 1952 to create a school for their children with cerebral palsy, for whom getting an education in those days was "harder than entering the kingdom of heaven". By 1960, the Society had created 120 local groups and 70 centres and schools.

My father wrote, "In twelve years, quite a number of the projects fought for so passionately at that first meeting in 1952 have been achieved. But still the more that is done, the more new needs are discovered. There seems no limit to what must be attempted if the money can be raised. As yet the Society has but scratched the surface."

The title of the book, *Every Eight Hours*, referred to how often a child was born with cerebral palsy in the UK. Despite recent improvements in medical science, the incidence of cerebral palsy has altered little over the years and the need for an organisation such as Scope has, if anything, grown, as babies with more severe impairments are surviving into adulthood.

As Scope celebrates its 50th anniversary, it seems a suitable moment to reflect.

Fifty years ago, there was widespread ignorance of cerebral palsy. There was nowhere for parents to go for support. Now, thousands of families get the support they can't find elsewhere by calling Scope's free CP Helpline.

Fifty years ago, children with cerebral palsy were branded 'ineducable'. Now, 350 young people attend Scope's six schools and college, and many more go to mainstream schools with Scope's support.

Fifty years ago, very few disabled people had full-time employment. Now, Scope supports hundreds of disabled adults into jobs each year.

Fifty years ago, adults with cerebral palsy either lived in their parents' homes or were sent to long-stay hospitals where they had little privacy or independence. Now, Scope supports 600 disabled adults to lead the lives they choose in independent accommodation and residential units.

Although much has been achieved, there is still so much to be done before disabled people achieve equality. This history is different in one very important aspect: it is written by

Foreword

Chris Davies, a journalist with cerebral palsy whose mother attended the first meeting of the National Spastics Society in 1952. I had the pleasure of working with Chris when he joined the team of my ITV Network political show, *Jonathan Dimbleby*. He was a powerful contributor to our lively pre-programme discussions. It is no surprise to me, therefore, that *Changing Society* pulls few punches; it contains a range of experiences of and opinions about the organisation. It is indeed a personal history, both for Chris and for his 17 interviewees, many of whom, like Chris, are disabled people. This reflects a major change in Scope itself: in 1952, The National Spastics Society ruling executive had one person with cp, Bill Hargreaves; now, Scope's Executive Council has a majority of disabled people. It's just one way that Scope is changing society.

I hope you enjoy reading Chris's book. I have found it stimulating, illuminating and inspired by a will and purpose which would, I know, have delighted my father 50 years ago.

Changing Society

Hilda Davies with the author

Introductions

In 1952, when Scope (formerly The Spastics Society) was born, I was six years old. I have no real memory of my parents' active involvement in those early days of the organisation, but I dimly remember travelling from the north-west to London and sleeping in the office of the Society founder Ian Dawson-Shepherd.

The next memories I have are of my parents seeking local authorities to enable me to attend, eventually, a grammar school in Kent run by the Society. From these memories to the present day stretches my lifetime's association with what we now know as Scope.

I owe the organisation much, because it has provided me with essential education, accommodation and employment. Through my association, I am very conscious of the benefits given to countless people with cerebral palsy (cp). Nevertheless, I am also aware that the organisation, just like the people within it, is far from perfect. It is my intention to see Scope as it was, as it is, and as it could or should be. The very fact that many of

Changing Society

those featured in this book have a close association with Scope probably means that objectivity is at a premium. Yet this book is not meant to be a spotless portrayal. Of course, it will also show the good side but, if it is accurate, it will also illustrate those aspects of Scope that are still not as they should be.

Who is the cast of *Changing Society*? There are, of course, representatives of the triangle of constituencies that have always been, and remain, the core of Scope – parents, people with cerebral palsy and professionals. They represent the five decades of Scope's life. Whatever their association with Scope, they have an interesting story to tell and strong opinions to relate.

After this initial chapter, the book is comprised of five sections, each containing individuals' views about a decade of Scope's existence. Preceding each section, there will be key dates for each decade in Scope's development. When the story has reached the present day, the final chapter will concern itself with the views of all those in the book about the future of Scope and its ongoing role.

One of the founders, Alex Moira

William Burn

Given the historical fact that Scope was born out of parental concern that children with cerebral palsy were not being given adequate provision, it is only appropriate that my list of participants begins with two survivors from the founding days. My own mother and father were amongst those early activists. My father died in 1971, but my mother, **Hilda Davies**, is still very much active. I don't think I have ever been told the full story of her role in Scope. I am only aware that it was very difficult to obtain interest from the public in the new organisation. I have no way of knowing how typical my mother's story is, but I do know that what she did and why she did it are at the very core of Scope's story.

My mother is not the sole representative of the earliest days of Scope. **Bill Hargreaves**, for many, must be the epitome of Scope. A man with cerebral palsy who was on the first Executive Council, then later a member of staff, he has certainly been in the public eye for most of Scope's life. With Bill on the earliest Executive Councils was **Alex Moira**, who was one of four founding members at the historic meeting in 1951 when The Spastics Society was conceived. **William Burn**, like Alex, a parent of a child with cerebral palsy, was also active in these

Bill Hargreaves at Scope's AGM in 1998   PHOTO: GILL SHAW

Changing Society

pioneering times, eventually becoming Chairman.

You will probably not know my mum's name, even if you are very well acquainted with Scope, but the representative of the second generation of Scope parents probably needs no introduction to you. **Anthony Hewson**, as chair of the organisation from 1990 to 1997, saw The Spastics Society through its momentous name change to its birth as Scope in 1994. I cannot claim to know him well, but from my acquaintance with him, I think his chairmanship was a great learning experience for him. He, like my mum, has a son with cerebral palsy, **Toby Hewson**, who represents the future of Scope and has probably benefited from his father's association with **Glynn Vernon** (also in these pages). Did Anthony's perspective change from that of a typical parent filled with foreboding of what his son will encounter during his life, to a more liberating perspective which contemplated Toby's independence?

If anyone reading this book is unfamiliar with the structure of the organisation, perhaps I should explain something. Virtually all the people interviewed have an association with

Anthony Hewson with son Toby

Glynn Vernon

Introductions

Scope that is purely voluntary. Members of the Executive Council, even the Chairman, do not receive any financial reward. Among the people in this book, there are just five exceptions. Bill Hargreaves used to work as industrial liaison officer, charged with gaining meaningful employment for disabled people. I, at one time, worked in the PR department at Park Crescent, the Society's Head Office. Currently **Alison John** works as a Disability Equality Trainer on an occasional basis for Scope. The other two people need special mention because both are ex-Chief Executives who were in charge of the day-to-day running of the organisation. **Sir John Cox**, previously a Vice-Admiral, now works with other voluntary organisations. **Tim Yeo** left the Society in 1983 to become a Conservative MP and later a member of the Shadow Cabinet.

My secondary education was in the only grammar school for people with cerebral palsy, Thomas Delarue School in Tonbridge, Kent. Two of my contemporaries there are included in these pages. The first has already been mentioned. Glynn Vernon and I spent most of our teenage years together. You may remember a disability awareness video made by Scope called

Sir John Cox
PHOTO: MICHELLE SMITH

Alison John in 1981
PHOTO: MARGARET MURRAY

Tim Yeo

Changing Society

Stand Up The Real Glynn Vernon. He is, by inclination, a political radical and a plain speaker, and as member of Executive Council since 1989 and a former Vice Chairman, he is in a strong position to discuss Scope past, present and future. The other is **Andrew Berry**, who was also a member of the Executive Council and claims to be the person who initiated the word 'Scope' as a potential new name for the organisation.

The first woman with cerebral palsy on Executive Council, **Valerie Lang**, like Glynn, is another ex-Vice Chair of Scope. As with Bill Hargreaves, Valerie is also very publicly associated with the organisation.

Andy Berry

Valerie Lang

So far, this list is of people who have a very close association with Scope. However, just to confine a book in this way would be wrong. Scope has many critics, not least those disabled people who consider it to be over-conservative and over-paternalistic. I have met many of these critics and I would not disagree with much that they say. Regrettably, a large number of these critics offer viewpoints that are not informed by personal knowledge of Scope. This does not apply to Alison John. Alison has been the subject of four major documentaries, made by the BBC about her life as a disabled woman and her uneasy relationship with The Spastics Society. Despite her freelance training work for Scope, this has not blunted her outspoken views.

Introductions

Poet and performer **Rosamund Browne** also went to Thomas Delarue grammar school, and is active as a celebrity supporter with the Stars Organisation for Scope (SOS), but is nevertheless somewhat critical of all charities, not least Scope.

Finally, in this group, **Alan Martin** who is active in Merseyside with Scope, but who is nevertheless critical.

Rosamund Browne

Of the people in this book, there are only three I had not met prior to its writing. All three have cerebral palsy but their backgrounds are very different. **Pat Entwistle** is a writer, the author of *What's in a Life?* Pat's main area of activity is transport and his home ground, like mine, is in the north-west of England. **John Queenborough** is also another author, but his work charts the sea change in the lifestyle of those who are now venturing into independent living. John was a resident of The Princess Marina Centre, the Scope residential community that is now being replaced by individual accommodation to enable him and his friends to be free of the restrictions of institutionalisation. Although not much of my life has been spent in any kind of institutional environment,

Alan Martin

Pat Entwistle

I nevertheless have some experience of it, and am aware of how difficult it must be, suddenly to be independent. John's experiences are crucial because they are very much related to the evolution of Scope's practices.

I don't really like using the phrase 'last but not least' when it introduces **Angela Smith**. There is nothing about Angela's life or opinions that should make her last on anyone's list. She is disabled, but the perspective that makes her viewpoint particularly significant is that she is black. Angela and I have discussed the cultural perspective of disability many times. If Scope is not to become a one-dimensional organisation, learning from people such as Angela is crucial.

John Queenborough

That's my cast. It can't be entirely comprehensive, but it should offer some interesting insights into a breathing entity and its changes over 50 years.

As I begin, I am anticipating a very interesting journey of discovery. Although, as I have said, my association with Scope is close and long, there will be aspects that I'm sure will surprise me. I hope that the book will clarify the manner in which Scope has evolved. It is often assumed that little has changed about Scope, but this has to be wrong, everything changes in time.

Angela Smith

The only certainty I have before meeting anyone is that Scope has undoubtedly changed in the course of 50 years. But has it changed for the better? Is it still serving the purpose for which it was originally established, and, at the onset of the new century, is it still credible and viable?

Scope is aimed at changing society. Has it? Does it? Will it? Read on.

Fifties

1946	1949	1951	1952	1952
St. Margaret's, a residential school for children with cerebral palsy, opened in Croydon. **The British Council for the Welfare of Spastics** (BCWS) formed.	**The Dame Hannah Rogers School** opened.	9 October – The organisation now known as Scope was founded by a group of parents.	5 January – Inaugural meeting of the **National Spastics Society** (NSS).	The **Percy Hedley School**, Newcastle opened. The Society's first residential unit, **Coombe Farm** opened in Croydon.

Key Dates 1946-1959

1955	1956	1957	1958	1959
	It was reported there are 30,000 people with cerebral palsy in the UK.		The Society's AGM voted to receive funds from a football pools scheme. **Daresbury Hall**, a residential service, and **Hawksworth Hall**, an assessment centre, opened.	
The Society opened three schools and Prested Hall (later Drummonds). **SOS** (the Stars Organisation for Spastics) was founded. The BCWS opened Ponds Residential Centre (now **Princess Marina Centre**).		The Society employed an Employment Officer, **Margaret Morgan,** and an Industrial Liaison Officer, **William Hargreaves.**		The Society moved to **12 Park Crescent**. Merger talks with BCWS began.

Changing Society

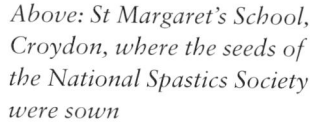

Above: St Margaret's School, Croydon, where the seeds of the National Spastics Society were sown

Centre: The founder's daughter, Rosemary Dawson-Shepherd, at St Margaret's

Below: Valerie Lang was also a pupil at St Margaret's

The 1950s, Beginnings

1952. That is when it all began... isn't it?
Well, yes... On 5 January 1952, at the Ambassador Hotel in Southampton Row, London, representatives from 14 groups of people with cerebral palsy met, and formally inaugurated an organisation to be called The National Spastics Society (NSS). But that's not where the story really begins, because as with most entities, the organisation we now know as Scope had a gestation period which pre-dates 1952.

If the inaugural meeting was the 'birth', the 'conception' took place on 9 October 1951. The place was Long Lane, Croydon. The main participants, those considered to be the founders of the organisation, were three parents of children with cerebral palsy, all of whom went to the same school, and a social worker from that school. The parents were Ian Dawson-Shepherd, Alex Moira and Eric Hodgson. The social worker, whose wealthy family owned the premises on which the school was built, was Jean Garwood. The four, together with legal advisor John Tomlinson, discussed and decided to create a society that would provide better provision for their children and others like them.

Until I began my research, I was under the impression that the main reason for setting up the NSS was because there was nothing that catered for this section of the population. Not so. Yes, disabled people generally, and people with cerebral palsy in particular, had nowhere near the high profile they have today. Very little had been done, but not nothing. The school that the children of the founders attended (and where the social worker worked) was St. Margaret's and was opened in September 1946. The British Council for the Welfare of Spastics (BCWS) was then constituted at a meeting held on 17 October 1946. However, even before this, an organisation existed which specialised in cerebral palsy. The British Council was the brainchild of Henry Weston, who had earlier co-founded the Association for the Care of Sufferers of Cerebral Palsy, an organisation consisting mainly of parents. BCWS, co-founded by another parent, Leslie Williams was originally intended to be a parent-led body.

Although the BCWS had existed for six years before Scope's founders had met at Eric Hodgson's home, there was much dissatisfaction. From the beginning, professionals dominated the Council and the main objective was medical research. Therefore, the St Margaret's parents' dissatisfaction was because they wanted more concrete assistance in the provision of education, accommodation and employment for their children. That is why the BCWS was not seen as being enough, and that is why the group meeting in Croydon wanted to create something better – and did so, with the National Spastics Society.

But the story goes back even further. Henry Weston met Leslie Williams in 1943 when he visited a physiotherapist, Eirene Collis, at an experimental Cerebral Palsy Unit at Queen Mary's Hospital, Carshalton. Weston had been put in contact with Collis through Dr Winthrop Phelps, who had established the

Beginnings

first specialist clinic for children with cerebral palsy in 1920 in the United States. Is 1920 the start of the start of the story? Yes, if 'the story' is simply the chain of events that led to Scope. But that is only tracing the history of organisations and the individuals involved. This ignores the fact that the condition of cerebral palsy itself has a history. For example, the condition has had numerous name changes. More recently, debate has centred on the words 'spastic' or 'cerebral palsy'. Strictly speaking, 'spastic' refers to only one form of cerebral palsy. Before this, the condition was known as 'spastic paralysis' and before that, 'infantile paralysis'. The first name, though, was Little's Disease, so called because the first scientific description of the condition was given by Dr WJ Little in 1861. Even though I can remember that in the Bible, Christ cured someone who was 'sick of the palsy', I think that is about as far as I shall go!

That's the background, now to work forward. At the 1951 meeting of parents in Croydon, what happened?

Well, they formed themselves into a properly constituted committee. They adopted their St Margaret's Parents Committee roles: Ian Dawson-Shepherd as Chairman; Eric Hodgson as Secretary; Alex Moira as Treasurer and Jean Garwood as Advisor. Apparently, there was then some debate about what they should call themselves. Ian Dawson-Shepherd strongly favoured the word 'spastic' in the title, but Eric Hodgson and Alex Moira both favoured 'cerebral palsy'. Jean Garwood agreed with the latter because she said, "It was the proper medical term." It seems to me an indication of the force of Dawson-Shepherd's character that three out of four people agreed the term 'cerebral palsy', and then decided on the title 'National Spastics Society'. Dawson-Shepherd, who worked in advertising, perceived the word 'spastic' as one that would catch the public's imagination. Well, if that was the case, it

Changing Society

The 1951 meeting as re-enacted in the NSS film 'Every Eight Hours'

certainly did not do so for some time, as we shall see.

But it is evident that at this meeting Ian Dawson-Shepherd was supremely confident. He pulled out a £5 note saying, "That's a start." Eric Hodgson is reported to have said, "A fiver won't get us very far." Undaunted, Ian Dawson-Shepherd replied, "All right then, I'll make you a million pounds in five years." Eric responded, "Don't talk bloody daft."

Alex Moira would readily admit that his memory of that day is not clear. But he has clear memories of how that meeting came about. *"I was involved before the original Spastics Society was first formed, due to my dissatisfaction with the education available for my daughter, and, similarly, Ian Dawson-Shepherd and Eric Hodgson had the same problem and the same dissatisfaction. Our girls were all at the same school. My daughter was dismissed from that school because of the dissidence of her parents, and so we formed a society, mainly under the impetus of Dawson-Shepherd."*

This is how Alex Moira described that first meeting, *"I think we were rather excited. We each took a £5 note out of our pockets – and a £5 note was quite a large note in those days – particularly for a struggling architect, and put it on the table, as being the first finances."*

The group moved quickly, registered themselves as a charity and tried to raise interest, and of course, money, for the project which was at the root cause of their meeting in the first place – a better school for children with cerebral palsy. The Chairman wrote leaflets outlining aims and objectives of the embryonic organisation and distributed them widely, hoping to gain publicity. Among the people he contacted were the creators of a popular daily column *Live Letters* in *The Daily Mirror*. The paper agreed to publish his letter:

"A new and powerful society has been formed to press, argue and fight to get better treatment for spastic sufferers. Would you ask all sufferers or their relatives to write to the National Spastics Society at the above address and start helping the Society?"

The response? More than 300 replies from parents of children with cerebral palsy. That would not, on the face of it, appear to be a very huge return, but it has to be remembered that this was in answer to an organisation about which no one had heard previously. It also meant that there were more than 300 people who could start local groups, and Eric Hodgson quickly invited each to do just that. Now at last, the organisation could begin to be 'national'.

But, writing to people who share a common concern does not make an organisation. Meeting people who share this concern does. Hence the meeting held at the Ambassador's Hotel. Present were the representatives from St Margaret's School

Changing Society

Parents Association, Puckle Hill, Bexleyheath, Pinner, Reading, Buckinghamshire, Nottingham, Coventry, Cardiff, Newcastle, Leeds, Huddersfield and Wallasey.

The meeting agreed five guidelines, which later became the basic aims and objectives of the society. They were:

1 *To provide and promote facilities for the treatment, training, education and residential care of men, women and children with cerebral palsy.*

2 *To foster understanding of cerebral palsy as a disorder, and to help towards the acceptance of people with cerebral palsy in their homes and by society.*

3 *To provide help and support for disabled people and their families.*

4 *To show how authorities at all levels can and should help people with cerebral palsy.*

5 *To promote research into the causes, treatment and prevention of cerebral palsy.*

I've spoken to three people who were at that meeting. Alex Moira, of course, was there. My own mother was there. And so, too, was someone with cerebral palsy who actually spoke at that meeting. There have been differing accounts. Alex Moira told me, "*I think we hired a room for it, because we hadn't a room big enough, but that would only have put the number at 40 or 50.*"

For my mother the meeting was the beginning of a lifelong association with the organisation. This is how she describes it: "*I first became involved in 1952. I heard about it because we'd investigated joining the Welfare of Spastics Organisation [BCWS], so we went down to London, to the first meeting, chaired by*

Ian Dawson-Shepherd and with the other three that were the founders with him. It was a very good meeting. I can't really remember how many were there. I should think probably anything between 50 and 75ish. As far as my memory serves me, we were going to meetings of the NAPBC (National Association of Parents of Backward Children), and I think it was at a meeting when we took our children with us and I think it was discussed there. One of us, Edna, (who had a little boy aged about three at the time), Ethel Woods, and my husband and I decided to go to London to see what this was about."

The third person was William Hargreaves, known to everyone who knows Scope as Bill, and he has the unique distinction of being the only person with cerebral palsy to be involved in the formation of the organisation. He is a natural storyteller, so here, quite simply, is his description of how it all began.

"When I first became involved, it was way back in March 1952, when a parent from St Margaret's School, Croydon, which was then the only school for cerebral palsied children in the country, approached me, asking if I could help him and his son, and did I know about this new Society which was just starting up?

"Laurie Green knew about me because, during the latter part of the war, I was the Warden of a YMCA Forces Transit Hostel in Kettering, Northamptonshire. During that time he came as a soldier passing through, and he stayed at my hostel and recognised that his son had the same condition that I had.

"One day when I... came to my front door there were some leaflets and the leaflets bore the inscription 'Please help Spastics. What is a Spastic? It might have been your child.' It was 'It might have been your child' which I considered to have been the most potent message that they could have put across."

When Bill received the leaflets, he lost no time in getting

Bill Hargreaves was the Society's first Industrial Liaison Officer

involved, "*I went straight around, within the hour to Laurie Green's house, and I saw before me a child who was me. He told me that I was the first person they'd heard of who'd made it in life, and please, please could I help?*

"*We decided to set up a group forthwith. He asked me if I would chair it, and I became Chairman of the Corby group. A few weeks later the central committee, in other words, the National Spastics Society Executive Committee, held a meeting in Northampton. After that, I had a letter from Eric Hodgson, the first Secretary of The Spastics Society, saying that the Council wished to co-opt me onto this very first Council of The National Spastics Society. I was a co-opted member because they headhunted me, as it were. So it was totally by accident that they found me. And I was totally appalled that there wasn't anybody else."*

Around the same time, my parents were involved with their local group. This created a difficulty. This is how my mother describes it: *"Unfortunately, we lived in Liverpool in 1952 and the Liverpool Spastics Fellowship, in which my husband and I were active, would not affiliate [to the NSS]. I addressed meetings all over Merseyside and the Wirral; I collected at Lime Street Station at Christmas, the Liverpool Boxing Stadium and pubs on Saturday night."*

For many years (some would say too many years) parents ran the organisation. I wondered how Bill Hargreaves felt being the only disabled person in this situation. Although he has a realistic appreciation of the extent to which parents of disabled children can be overprotective, he vigorously defends the role of parents in the evolution of the organisation:

"The National Spastics Society would not have taken off if it had not been for the drive of the parents. It was the drive that was important. Of course, it was difficult for them as parents to realise their children must grow up and that there were various stages in their growing up. They were concerned with their children.

"Another section, the older ones, were concerned about their teenage sons and daughters and therefore the first result of the parents was to create schools. The second result was to create care homes, because parents became too old or decrepit to look after their sons or daughters properly, so they needed the comfort in their own mind of knowing they would be secure. Of course, they were paternalistic. Any parent is going to be paternalistic, but there was a person called Bill Hargreaves, and eventually a lot of others who were able to try and say 'Please

let go', and I created many enemies by saying that, and I don't deny that. Of course I did. You can't go forward in life without creating mayhem at times, when you're in our sort of work."

My parents have always led me to believe that their intention, in helping to form the organisation, was that, one day, with education provided by the organisation, I would be equipped, together with other people with cerebral palsy, to take on the work, which they started. It would seem that my parents were not typical, because, for many years, disabled people were conspicuously absent. I asked Bill about this.

"I remember getting up at an AGM many years ago now, don't ask me how many, and one person asked, 'Why aren't there any cerebral palsied people on the Executive Council?' And there was a deathly hush, and then I got up – and remember that that was a brave thing for me to do – I was then on the staff. I got up and said, 'Ladies and gentlemen, because you haven't put them there.' And that shook 'em. And the next person [with cerebral palsy] on the Executive Council, 15 years after me, was Adrian Wright, who was a solicitor.

"You see, I think the big problem was – and you can see this loud and clear with hindsight – anyone can have hindsight – was that it took that time for people with young cerebral palsied children to go through an education system which was not there when the Society started – it was the Society that had to put it in place – for the parents to then realise 'Oi, look what we've done! They're educated, and they can now come onto the Executive', and that, I think, is the real reason. They could not see [it was] because people in the Society weren't coming forward…"

Five days before the inaugural meeting, Sheila Rawstorne became the first paid employee of The National Spastics Society. The second was George Lauder, who was appointed General Secretary. The Society had staff but no offices, so Ian Dawson-

Shepherd would meet Sheila at 8 o'clock every morning in the Lyons teashop over Hammersmith Underground Station.

As she lived in Barnes and he drove past Hammersmith every morning, this very unusual working arrangement suited them both. Over tea and toast they would deal with the day's correspondence before he went on his way to his office in a Mayfair advertising agency, while she returned to her flat to type the letters and make the occasional phone call. In the evening she would return to the teashop for another session, or go to Alex Moira's house in Kensington to take the minutes of a committee meeting.

With Sheila Rawstorne working at her typewriter in her small flat, and George Lauder, whose office was either his lodgings or his battered old car, the fledgling organisation struggled. Money was hard to raise because no one knew of the Society. Then came a breakthrough.

The creators of *Live Letters* had been impressed with the letter they published about the new organisation and were willing to help further. They introduced Ian Dawson-Shepherd to the artist who drew the *Mirror*'s daily cartoon strip, *Ruggles*, about a fictitious suburban couple interested in social issues. Mr and Mrs Ruggles were the *Mirror*'s social conscience. So early in May 1952, *The Daily Mirror* gave its 15 million readers six days of a factual, easily understood view about children with cerebral palsy. At last, people knew about the condition.

On 30 September 1952, the first film commissioned by the organisation, *The Chance of Their Lives,* written by Ian Dawson-Shepherd and the distinguished journalist James Cameron, and introduced by the popular radio star Wilfred Pickles, was shown to the media and disability organisations. In February 1953, it was shown to MPs. Gradually the message was spreading.

Changing Society

In 1952 the Daily Mirror's Ruggles cartoon strip brought the work of The National Spastics Society to 15 million readers

In October, Ian Dawson-Shepherd reshaped the society's single-page newsletter and relaunched it as *The National Spastics News*, with a circulation of 5,000, sent direct to every group member, and to MPs, town clerks, Lord Mayors and heads of local authorities, editors of all the national newspapers, BBC radio and television.

By December 1952, 38 affiliated local groups had been established. At the first AGM in 1953 there were 60 affiliated local groups.

By October 1953, after Sheila Rawstorne had been forced to move twice by landlords annoyed by the clatter of her typewriter, the Society bought its first administrative office, a four-storey building, with a self-contained five-roomed flat on the top floor, at 44 Stratford Road, Kensington. My mum recalls this flat because she, and my father with me, stayed there. They were anxious to try a form of physiotherapy known as the Bobath method, and this was the reason for the trip. This is how she described it, *"I went to the Bobaths' flat, and to do that, my husband and myself and my cerebral palsied son stayed in what was then the headquarters of The Spastics Society in Stratford Road, London. Chris slept in Ian Dawson-Shepherd's bed, to be truthful with you. We went to the Bobaths' flat with Ian Dawson-Shepherd and Dr Polani, to see pictures of their work in Hungary."*

With increasing overheads, raising funds was vital. The first appeal letter by Ian Dawson-Shepherd was not a success. He sent over 1,000 letters addressed to the chairmen and managing directors of advertising agents, newspapers and printers. It raised exactly £310.8.0. And so the Society decided to hire a professional fundraiser. The man they appointed, Arthur Hersee, had mixed success. After some false starts, he decided to borrow an idea from another charity. He suggested selling charity seals. He showed the executive committee a sheet of Marie Curie Foundation Christmas Shields, and suggested that the Society copy the idea. It was agreed to spend £400 making seals depicting Westminster Abbey, which could be sold to coincide with the Coronation in June. Initially, the response was not encouraging, but then the organisation was swamped with requests for seals. By the end of August 1953, over £5,000 had been received, and two out of every three seals dispatched had been sold. As we will see, this success also caused difficulties.

However, even before the windfall of the seals in August, the organisation was in funds. At the second annual Congress held at Northampton on 17 January 1953, the Treasurer Alex Moira announced that since the formation of the Society, nearly £13,000 had been raised, chiefly by the sterling efforts of the parents' groups. A capital investment of £4,000 had been made, and after expenditure on seals and other fundraising efforts, he had a working balance in excess of £2,000.

The success of the Coronation seals had given Ian Dawson-Shepherd the idea that this was a potentially lucrative source of revenue. So he proposed to undertake a similar exercise for Christmas that year. He wanted to use the £5,000 income from the last seals campaign to make more money for the Society by printing 10 million 1953 Christmas seals and to spend even more money on publicity, which would in time produce more funds.

The proposal was not met with enthusiasm. The Executive Committee wanted to use the money from the first seals to buy property to house new projects. They only authorised the production of five million seals. The Chairman went away and immediately ordered the production of 10 million at a cost of £3,500 with three months' credit. A complication arose (there was no money for stamps!) and the Treasurer had

Changing Society

to be told. Only a week previously Alex Moira had told Ian Dawson-Shepherd that he had firmly committed the Society's funds (in accordance with the Executive Committee's ruling) to buy a building for use as a school. Nevertheless, the Chairman prevailed and the gamble paid off. Within four months £28,000 had been received. It was later declared that the final result of this campaign was that expenses had amounted to £8,000 but the gross income totalled £35,000. But this was not to be the only time that Ian Dawson-Shepherd gambled and took risks, almost at the expense of his relationship with the organisation. Dawson-Shepherd was playing for high stakes – he sincerely believed that a million pounds in five years was not only achievable, but vital if the organisation was to have any chance of changing the lives of people with cerebral palsy.

Motivated by the success of the Christmas seals, he wanted to print 120 million seals at an estimated cost of £33,000, backed up by an advertising campaign, spread over two months, costing £75,000. The financial sub-committee was aghast. He hastily added that it was his intention to ask the local groups to fund the cost of the advertising by means of a loan; between them they held that in their banks. He would ask them to pledge the £75,000 at the next general meeting.

The Society's Christmas seals, an early fundraising success, could have spelled ruin for the fledgling charity

Although the AGM appeared to welcome the idea, the next meeting of the Executive Council was less approving: £75,000 was practically every penny that the groups possessed – all to be spent in one advertising fling. The treasurer Alex Moira

Beginnings

Ian Dawson-Shepherd

produced figures that proved that with the expenditure already agreed by committee, the society would soon be some £7,000 in the red. An emphatic 'No' was unanimously voted to the proposal.

So Dawson-Shepherd revised his plan. He dropped the idea of an advertising campaign, but retained the intention to find £33,000 to print the seals. Once again he gambled, not just on the success of the seals, but also on the hope that the organisation would forgive his unilateral action. He struck a deal with a printer but delayed telling anyone until it was too late to withdraw. When he did, the reactions were something he long remembered. This is how he later described it in his memoir, *"To this day I remember the gasp, the look of appalled incredulity on the suddenly white faces of the executive members."*

Having already taken risks, he then took another with his own career: he told his audience that he would resign his advertising agency job and work full-time for the Society as a volunteer until the money came in. He imposed only one condition. He must remain Chairman and control the operation throughout. It must be a testimony to the value that they placed on his worth that, even given this audacity, they accepted his suggestion. A month later Jean Garwood came forward with an offer to pay him the same salary that he had earned at the agency for six months. It was an offer he promptly accepted very gratefully: he was not a wealthy man.

Of course, this was not the end of the gamble. He had persuaded the organisation not to prevent the production of the seals and to enable him to take overall control of the operation, but, if the seals failed to sell, his risk-taking would have been in vain. It wasn't, though. At the AGM on 2 July 1955, it was announced that a total of £250,000 had been raised.

1955 was a milestone in my life. In that year, my family moved across the Mersey to the Wirral. This move meant my mother was less involved with the organisation. Even before leaving Liverpool, she herself had felt a sense of distance between parents in the north-west and the so-called 'National' Society. In her words, *"We moved to Wirral in 1955 and I joined the Birkenhead organisation, but I was only required to help in their small schools, which had been founded and funded with Scope funds, and I was only doing cleaning and feeding... I have to say that, because I was so involved with what was happening with my own son, I perhaps wasn't so aware of what was happening nationally. Because we lived up north and the organisation was based in London, it always seemed to us to be a southern organisation and we were on the periphery, so perhaps we were not aware of the things that were going on down south at the headquarters."*

So why was there a gap? I asked. *"Because of the mileage between us and because most of us who were eager to do things were parents of cerebral palsied children. There was nowhere to leave them while we went down south to meetings. The National Spastics Society was set up by parents, of course, and they wanted to raise £1 million to enable the centres they were going to set up for treatment and education, and we were very thrilled about this: this was what we wanted. But there were others in Liverpool anyway, who weren't that interested and we had a bit of a problem with that. When we moved to Birkenhead, they were still a bit isolated."*

In 1955, many of the recognisable features of the organisation were started. Number 28 Fitzroy Square opened as a new headquarters, housing projects such as employment, appeals and social work. A residential centre, Prested Hall, now called Drummonds, opened in Colchester. The Society also opened Wilfred Pickles School in Rutland, Craig-y-Parc School near Cardiff and, what was then, the first-ever grammar school for disabled children anywhere, Thomas Delarue School at Tonbridge, Kent.

In 1957, an 11-year-old boy called Christopher Davies would begin five years there. Already at the school was Glynn Vernon, and soon to join me there, Andrew Berry and Rosamund Browne, all of whom are contributors to this book. Also among my contemporaries were Rosemary Dawson-Shepherd, Alice Moira and Graham Burn, whose fathers all feature so heavily in the story of Scope.

In 1957, Dr Charles Stevens, the first Director, was appointed in March. In addition, Bill Hargreaves was persuaded to leave the voluntary work of the Executive Committee to become the first Industrial Liaison Officer. This is how it happened in his words, *"I was asked to be Chairman of the Employment Sub-committee and the Sub-committee brought into being Sherrards Industrial Training Centre and then looked around*

Changing Society

Top: *Thomas Delarue School, 1959*

Above: *Glynn Vernon in 1959*

Right: *The author (front left) on a school visit to London Zoo in October 1958*

for what it should be doing next. I said, 'We need an Employment Officer.'"

The Society, with Bill in the chair of the interview panel, appointed Margaret Morgan as Employment Officer. Bill, it turned out, was appointing his own boss! He continues:

"Ian Dawson-Shepherd had given me a very liquid lunch and he said; 'Now Bill, I want you to do a job. I want you to go into industry to do PR, to get jobs for spastics.' I said, 'You must be joking.' But this was the vision, and the vision I had actually. That all these teenagers needed employment help.

"My brief was to go out into industry and win hearts and minds so that people would be prepared to employ our people."

In 1958, Francis Van Neste and Douglas Arter proposed to the Society a national football pools competition with a weekly subscription of one shilling, two pence of which would go to The Friends of Spastics League and directly benefit the charity.

Alice Moira among a group of Delarue pupils watching Mr Pastry digging the first sod of earth for a new swimming pool, made possible by the comedy star's prodigious fundraising efforts

Changing Society

Associating the Society with gambling was controversial in some supporters' eyes, and the Midlands group representative stormed out of the AGM that accepted the proposal.

Within three months, £5,000 was coming weekly into the Society from the scheme; within six months, £10,000; a year later, £20,000 a week. Membership grew and at its peak reached 6.7 million people worldwide and raising over £2 million a year.

The money kept coming in, and the Society kept expanding, with Daresbury Hall, a residential service, and Hawksworth Hall, an assessment centre, both opening in June 1958.

Eric Hodgson was the first of the founders to leave. He resigned in 1958 because of his disagreement with certain current aspects of the Society's policy. He found it difficult to come to terms with what was to him, a complete change of direction of the Society with so much money being poured into bricks and mortar: *"The old, small, friendly approach has gone. Perhaps it should go, but if it doesn't come back I feel that I, too, ought to go."* He had little to do with the Society after he left. Eric Hodgson died in Yorkshire in 1976.

The final year of the Society's first decade was truly a landmark one. During 1959, it moved to a new headquarters at 12 Park Crescent, surely for many people the building that came to symbolise the organisation. The charity's increasing confidence and prosperity led to its endowment of the Professorship of Child Health Research – the first in the world – in conjunction with a £2 million programme of research into the causes of cerebral palsy. The Society also embarked on merger discussions with the British Council for the Welfare of Spastics and saw Dame Hannah Rogers and Percy Hedley Schools affiliate to it.

By the turn of the decade, I was beginning my third year at The Thomas Delarue School at the age of 14. I was starting to feel adult, having left my childhood. I suppose the same could be said about Scope at this time. It had put down roots, become a part of the public consciousness and now it needed to make good use of this. Everyone knows the Sixties were a decade of significant change for society in general, but how was it for the Society?

Changing Society

Beginnings

The SOS was a galaxy of stars

Sixties

1960	1961	1963	1963	1964
Jack Emms replaced Ian Dawson-Shepherd as the new Chairman. **Every Eight Hours** film launched.	**Ingfield Manor School** opened.		**William Burn** succeeded Alex Moira as Treasurer.	The BCWS and NSS merge to become The Spastics Society with **Dr Dennis Wheeler** in the Chair.	**Chester Skills Development Centre, White Lodge Centre** in Chertsey, **Wakes Hall Centre** in Essex and the Mount (later to become **Rutland House School** in Nottingham) opened. **Every Eight Hours**, written by Richard Dimbleby, is published.

Key Dates 1960-1969

1965	1966	1967	1968	1969
	Kyre Park residential service, **Gladys Holman Home** in Cornwall and **Meldreth School** opened.		**Fitzroy Square Family Service and Assessment Centre** and **Sully Skills Development Centre** opened.	
Broadstones residential service, **Meadway Works**, a sheltered workshop in Birmingham, and **Thorngrove Agriculture Centre** opened.		**James Loring** appointed as Chief Executive.		**Lancaster Training Centre** opened.

Changing Society

Selling the Society's 4,000,000th Christmas card

PHOTO: IAN CLOOK

The 1960s, Expansion

I hardly knew Ian Dawson-Shepherd. As a child, I met him on a few occasions, and later as an adult, when he was quite old. I don't remember him as particularly charismatic or dynamic, but clearly he was. As I have already shown he took great risks and might have alienated his colleagues but he was permitted to go ahead and the risks paid off. Fifty years on it appears that he dominated the organisation during the early years. Although it was founded by four people, if anyone is entitled to be called the 'father' of Scope it must surely be Ian Dawson-Shepherd.

Therefore it must have come as a great shock to learn he was considering leaving the organisation. In the spring of 1960 he had decided that it was time for him to resign the position of Chairman and membership of the Executive Committee of the Society. The pressures of being the chairman of a charity with a turnover of millions of pounds a year, in addition to the demands of being a top marketing executive for a multi-national company were having a detrimental effect on his

Changing Society

domestic life. The extent of the shock can be measured by the value placed upon him by his associates. At an extra-ordinary meeting, on 28 May, the Treasurer, Alex Moira, gave the following appreciation of one with whom he had been involved even before the formation of the Society:

"I find myself with a peculiarly difficult task. Firstly, I find it impossible to think formally of that warm and human personality that we know so well, and secondly, I find it difficult to express thanks adequate to the incomparable service and leadership that he has given over the years to the Society. He is a man who steadfastly refuses to be thanked or even accept the credit that is due to him. Perhaps we can solve this difficulty of expressing our thanks adequately in a somewhat indirect way by resolving that we will carry on the Society with the utmost self-discipline and achieve effectively those goals that he has set us and towards which he has led us so far. This then is the greatest tribute that we can offer in resolving to carry on with skill and devotion the enterprise that he started us on. Ever since I have known Ian, he has overworked himself with rare skill, never more than in recent months. It was with almost relief that I learned of his intention to take life somewhat more easily and to retire, for the time being, from active participation in the Society's affairs. Relief, but also with very great regret that we are to lose one whose courage and enthusiasm have carried us through the early teething troubles and sticky patches inseparable from a growing society."

So what exactly had he achieved? By 1960 there were 120 local groups, a secure financial base, a research fellowship, and amalgamation with the British Council was near. During his time the organisation had established 70 local and national centres and schools plus a college of further education.

Although his was a hard act to follow, someone had to do so.

Jack Emms, an actuary and a parent of a son with cerebral palsy, who was later to become the head of the Commercial Union insurance company, was elected into the Chair.

1960 saw the launch of a film that gave me my first consciousness of the organisation. My guess is that I was shown it at school since one of the people featured in it visited us quite frequently. He was Bill Hargreaves and although I have since learned that he had an interest in the employment prospects of the people at the school, his main role, as far as I can remember, was that of an entertainer. But more of that later. The film in which Bill featured was *Every Eight Hours* (a reference to the incidence of cerebral palsy among UK births at the time). I guess that for most of the people outside the organisation the distinguishing factor of the film was that it was introduced and narrated by Richard Dimbleby. Having broadcast in the war and commentated on events such as the Coronation, his name and indeed his voice gave anything with which he was associated an indelible stamp of unquestionable authority. The Society's film therefore couldn't fail to grab the attention of viewers.

Nevertheless my impression of the film at the time was that it was more than a little doom-laden, a bit like a public health warning against cerebral palsy! Bill's role was that of 'a spastic' speaking up. Very much a film of its day, nevertheless it gave me a sense of identity for the organisation and if it worked in this way for me it could equally well do so for others. And that, I would say, justifies it completely.

By 1960 Bill Hargreaves had been travelling the country spreading the message: *"Given the right chance, many disabled people could do a good job of work."*

After five years of travelling and 247 towns, having survived on glucose tablets between speaking engagements and often away from his young family, Bill felt *"like a walking tape recorder"*. However, he had placed over 1,500 people with cerebral palsy into their first jobs, and the influence of his work had spread far and wide. The Ministry of Labour published 10,000 copies of his speech to distribute to every one of its local committees, and his life story had been broadcast on BBC Radio as *Can You Manage Stairs?*

Bill recalls his next step:

"I was asked to look into how I could help with social skills, because my first report upon talking at the Thomas Delarue School was 'It's all very well giving people a piece of paper to say they've got an examination pass, but have you told them how to deal with buses? Have you taught them how to use an outside phone? Have you taught them how important it is to get the work done on time?' Then I started initiative courses, where we took people away a week at a time, to let them do their own housework, their own shopping, to go and buy train tickets – all these sort of things. I had them trailed so they didn't get into any trouble – they didn't know they were being trailed."

So that's what he was doing at my school! I find myself embarrassed at the thought that to me as a 12-year-old, he was just a middle-aged ventriloquist with a disability. How wrong can you be?

In 1962, Bill decided to do something about improving the social lives of people with cerebral palsy. He explains:

"The 62 Clubs began because we had a meeting of cerebrally palsied people at Park Crescent, a sort of get-together from some of the assessment courses, from people who lived in London and the London area, and we thought, 'Shall we have a club here?' and we decided, 'Yes, let's have a club. A do-it-yourself club. No helpers.' And what happened? They did it themselves. They were self-help groups for cerebrally palsied people.

The 62 Clubs gave the opportunity to disabled people to organise their own activities, including a cross-channel sailing

"The first breakthrough was when we had a cerebrally palsied Chairman, Secretary, Treasurer and so forth, and I had to teach all of them how to do those functions; and how to be a committee, how to come to a decision. The first thing they did, which was a breakthrough, was decided they wanted to go on an outing to Westcliffe-on-Sea. They said, 'We'd like you to order a bus.' I said, 'I'm not ordering a bus. You're the Secretary:

you order the bus.' (Gasp) 'They won't bite, you know. You pick up the phone.' So they ordered the bus and it pulled up outside Park Crescent and they realised that they couldn't get the wheelchairs on the bus. So they learned that way, you see. I used to get the local group to have a meeting to tell me who, amongst the cerebrally palsied members, they thought would be able to do something. So I would then talk to the group and when I'd spoken about the work I was wanting doing in the 62 Clubs I'd say, 'Now will all the able-bodied people and parents please go and enjoy a cup of tea in the other room while we now elect our own Chairman, Secretary and Committee?'"

Sad to say, this would be considered radical by some even today so just think what it must have seemed like at the time! Nevertheless the idea took off, so much so, that by February 1965 Bill presided over the first national conference of the clubs at which 35 members from 13 clubs attended. This was the first-ever conference organised by and for people with cerebral palsy in Britain. This was later followed by a world conference in November 1969.

After four years and 17 meetings between the British Council for the Welfare of Spastics and The National Spastics Society, Chairman Jack Emms told delegates at an extra-ordinary general meeting held in February 1963 that he believed the interests of people with cerebral palsy would be best served by one society. A working party recommended transferring the assets of the BCWS to the NSS, subject to The National Spastics Society changing its name to The Spastics Society. The name 'British Spastics Society' had been proposed, thus incorporating the two names, but as there already existed organisations for people with cerebral palsy in Scotland and in Northern Ireland, and as the initials BSS referred to an existing organisation, it was felt that the adjective 'British' was unacceptable. Another influential voice added his weight of authority towards the change. Ian Dawson-Shepherd, speaking from the floor, welcomed the amalgamation. He felt that the influx of new blood from the BCWS would be of considerable benefit to the new Society. On 9 February 1963 The National Spastics Society was reborn as The Spastics Society. This was not the last of the organisation's incarnations, as we shall see.

1963 was significant for another change. Alex Moira, one of the founding parents, resigned as Treasurer, because of the increasing pressures of his architectural practice, and because he firmly believed that the Society now needed a Treasurer with professional qualifications. This is how he described what happened:

"I was Treasurer for the first five years, and then I became the Vice-Chairman, with the responsibility for services, and I held that post through until 1981. When I ceased to be Vice-Chairman (I was voted out), I became a member of the Executive Council straightforwardly, and a couple of years after that, I resigned from the Society. I had already started the Housing Association, which was associated with The Spastics Society at that time [Habinteg], and that was absorbing my attention entirely. That's why I wanted to get out of the Society and reduce my commitments. Then there was the Irish Housing Association, which we branched off into, and we helped the Scottish Housing Association to get going, and there's a sort of loose group there, which is doing very, very good work."

His replacement was William Burn, another parent of a child with cerebral palsy. This is how he described to me the events that led up to his appointment:

"We heard about the Croydon Spastics, which had formed in 1952, the same time as the national Society. We immediately got involved, and met Jean Garwood, and my wife and I were

Changing Society

elected to the Executive Committee of the Croydon Society, and I was very busy, working overtime and travelling the world at that time, so I was only on the Executive Council with Jean Garwood's understanding as an advisor overall, on the scope and finances of the society.

"I carried on like that, and in 1959, I joined the Council and immediately was put on the Finance Committee, because of my business experience, and that was all I took on for the time being. We had quite a serious crisis within the Society, within six months of my joining, (about May the following year), and the Executive Council had to be shuffled: that's when Ian Dawson-Shepherd retired completely from the Council, and Jack Emms became Chairman, Alex Moira continued as Vice-Chairman and I was appointed Honorary Treasurer, and that's all within a few months of joining the Council."

Drummonds service-users sell their wares   PHOTO: CHEEK, ESSEX COUNTY STANDARD

In November 1963 the first Annual General Meeting of the new organisation was held. It was told that 600 further places in national schools and centres were to be made available over the next three years, to be increased by at least 600 in the following six years.

1963 for me was a time of freedom. I had just left Delarue School after five years and was looking forward to the prospect of not being separated from my parents for nine months of the year. The school, you see, was residential and I hated being away from home. I will never regret going there because it gave me the impetus for studying – eventually. For four of these years, despite being in the most intensive academic environment ever devised for disabled people, I had no incentive to learn, simply because I was given none. The 'powers-that-be' in the school decided that my natural intelligence was not worthy of nurturing, and so didn't bother to do so. At the end of the fourth year, they expected me to leave because I had gone as far as they thought it possible for me academically. Fortunately my parents objected and I was given an extra year and the opportunity to qualify for O-levels and A-levels. Suddenly there was a reason to study instead of just doing it as a chore and I realised that I enjoyed the challenge. It gave me a thirst for academic achievement that I pursued until the early Eighties. The other factor that improved was the social side of school life. Whereas previously I was on the fringe in terms of having friendships, within the final year, I suddenly found myself becoming popular. Delarue was definitely a mixed blessing.

The initial feeling of freedom after leaving did not last. I soon felt bored and wanted to pursue my studies. So I approached my local art college (Art Appreciation had been one of my favourite subjects at school). I was rejected because if I couldn't physically practise art they weren't interested in having me.

Changing Society

I then went on to study some more A-levels at technical college locally. My appetite grew so that my parents arranged for me to attend Oakwood Further Education College in Essex. Oakwood, like Delarue, is no longer part of Scope but it was devised as the natural successor to the school in Kent, so that bright, severely impaired pupils from Delarue could further their academic career after leaving. I was at Oakwood until 1971.

From 1964 onwards the organisation's main characteristic was that of expansion. Among the facilities which opened were Chester Skills Development Centre, White Lodge Centre for disabled children, Castle Priory training college, a new work centre at Bramley Hill, a residential service at Broadstones, Meadway Works, a sheltered workshop in Birmingham, Thorngrove Agriculture Centre and the Mount (later to become Rutland House School) in Nottingham. In addition, the celebrity fundraising arm of the organisation, SOS, opened Wakes Hall Centre in Essex.

The growth of facilities just went on and on. In 1966 these included Kyre Park residential service, The Gladys Holman Home in Cornwall and Meldreth Training School, purpose-built to cater for the needs of 120 children with severe learning difficulties aged from five to 16. In 1968 the openings included Fitzroy Square Family Service & Assessment Centre and Sully

Wakes Hall *Meldreth Manor School*

Expansion

The Society's Director James Loring at Buckingham Palace 1979
PHOTO: MARIA BARTHA

The Fitzroy Square assessment centre

John Queenborough

Skills Development Centre. This pattern continued until 1969 with the opening of Lancaster training centre.

This rate of expansion could not continue. I wonder if, in 1968 when the Executive Council appointed a new Chief Executive, James Loring, he suspected that he might have to exercise more than a little restraint.

For Rosamund Browne and John Queenborough, their involvement began in the Sixties. Rosamund now has connections with SOS but her association with the main organisation began like this: *"Scope have been in and out of my life. In 1964 I left an ordinary mainstream school to go to Delarue, which was when Scope featured again, and I left there with an A-level and five O-levels, and went on to teacher training college."*

John Queenborough's involvement was tied into where he was living. *"From 1960 onwards I went to Glengall Road… what they called a hostel in those days. Not really a hostel, they helped people and looked after people… It was rather mundane in the overall pattern of hostel life. My earliest memory was when I went to my assessment in 1961, that was a residential and I had never been away from home before. It was a remarkable experience."*

In the Sixties the Society not only bedded itself down but also took roots and blossomed. As the decade drew to a close, pruning seemed inevitable.

Sadly this chapter has to end in a way which nobody would have wished. On 3 October 2000, during the writing of this chapter, Bill Hargreaves passed away. When I interviewed him 18 months previously he said he was having physical difficulties and not long after he rang me to tell me that he had been diagnosed with cancer. The last time I saw him was at Scope's 1999 AGM in Blackpool where he was feeling bright and cheerful because of a remission. The last time I spoke to him was in the middle of August 2000 in a telephone conversation and even then he was his usual effervescent self.

Scope owes much to Bill Hargreaves. People with cerebral palsy owe much to him. Since the time I interviewed him for this book he has been so supportive of me that I, too, owe much to him. It is my hope and intention that this book will be an adequate testimony of his work and his life. I will miss him and so, I am sure, will Scope.

Expansion

The 'human tape recorder', Bill Hargreaves, in action

Seventies

1970	1971	1972	1973	1974
The Society opened its **first shop** in Sevenoaks.		Chiltern House re-named as **Jack Howarth House**.		Residential units in **Kingston** and **Harpenden** opened.
	Jean Garwood died.		Ponds became the **Princess Marina Centre**. Habinteg Housing Association launched. Dorrien Belson replaced William Burn as Chairman.	

Key Dates 1970-1979

1975	1976	1977	1978	1979
	TSS now had 100 shops.		The **Save a Baby** campaign launched followed by a survey, **The British Way of Birth**.	
Churchtown Farm field centre opened.		**Beech Tree House** opened. TSS's emphasis was switched to disability prevention.		**Joyce Smith** and **Tim Yeo** became Chair and Director. The Society had a record deficit (£823,000).

Changing Society

Not everyone loved the Society's collection boxes!   PHOTO: P JOHNSON

The Seventies, Being There

It was probably inevitable that, sooner or later, the brakes would have to be applied.

By 1969 The Friends of Spastics League had had 6.7 million members worldwide and had raised £37 million for the Society. As a result of the 1964 Finance Act, the Commissioners of Customs and Excise brought a 'betting duty' case against the pools company. This centred on the definition of the word 'voluntary' when related to the deduction of the twopence contribution to the Society. The case eventually was decided in the House of Lords, who ruled against the pools company. Later, Peter Broderick, who was the Company Secretary of the pools company, said: *"For years the cheque that we paid to the Commissioners hung in our bank manager's office; at £13,000,000 it was the biggest cheque he had ever handled."* The decision effectively lost the Society about £900,000, which had been reserved against the outcome of the legal action.

After almost 20 years of expansion, it was now time to take stock and hold back. By the beginning of the Seventies,

Changing Society

William Burn as Chairman was overseeing a very difficult situation. Having grown so rapidly, it was important not to lose the momentum of success, while at the same time not being excessive.

He described to me his memories of this period:

"We realised pretty soon that it had grown too fast... centres were being put up, money was pouring in from regional pools promotions: it's like going at 60 miles per hour in a 30 miles per hour limit. We had to balance these things: not slow the growth down, but make sure the money was there at the right time and that we were spending it in the right way: not just chucking it down on any proposed development. So we gradually got the internal organisation going and then it became that much stronger... It's a question of making sure, on the Appeals side that we raised enough money, and we could never have too much, and we also then had to spend that money wisely..."

It was also the start of a new philosophy amongst employees of the organisation: *"One of the things I stressed to the staff was: 'You've got to work as a business internally. You've got to be efficient,' because too many charities, first of all, employ staff and they don't pay them the rate for the job."*

William Burn's management style was different:

"My main involvement (because of my background as a chartered accountant and senior business positions), together with previous Chairmen, Jack Emms and Dennis Wheeler, was to ensure that the management structure of the Society was efficient and successful and (during the Seventies) being in the forefront of the campaign for a more beneficial taxation regime for charities. I also believed that, although the ends and objectives of a charity such as The Spastics Society were very different from a commercial business, it was imperative to run the Society internally as if it was a competitive business in order to generate

the revenue needed and to fulfil its charitable aims. I had a privately-held objective to make the Society the 'ICI of charities, but with a heart'. After all, in the background all the time was my personal desire to help people with cerebral palsy."

Against the background of this more business-like approach, it is perhaps not surprising that the first year of the new decade saw the opening of the first Society shop in Sevenoaks, Kent. 1970 was also the year that someone who was to become, and who remains, a role model and the embodiment of all the good things about Scope, became involved with the organisation. Valerie Lang's first association began like this:

"I became involved in about 1970 or 1971, when I rang Bill Hargreaves with a question, and he decided that I would be suitable to join the 62 Club… I decided very quickly that I was not club-able, so I didn't join in any social activities or any particular 62 Club, but I became the Secretary to the National Association of the 62 Clubs. I think I probably did that for a couple of years. Derek Lancaster-Gaye and Alex Moira, one or the other, decided to co-opt me onto the Resources Committee, which was a sub-committee of the Exec., and I served on it for a number of years. In 1978, I nominated Dr Ron Firman to stand for the Executive, and he got in at the first try, so in 1979, he returned the favour and I was elected to the Executive."

Despite the fact that Bill Hargreaves had already made his presence felt on the Council, members at the time nevertheless did not find it easy to accommodate Valerie.

"When I was elected to the Council, it was the first time ever that they had two Council members at the same time who had cerebral palsy, and I was the first woman with cerebral palsy to be elected. I found it difficult, in that not everybody could understand what I was saying, and they were not prepared to ask me to repeat it, and I found that extremely difficult.

Changing Society

They gave me credit, but I feel that if people don't feel that it is important to understand what I've said, they're undermining my role. I'm vain enough to think that what I say matters, particularly in committees, because I make it a rule not to say anything at all in committees, unless I feel strongly and unless I feel the point hasn't been made before. I do know that it took me quite some time to establish my reputation with all of the Executive.

"The first time I attended a Society AGM, there were only about two of us there who had a disability. The lunch was set out as a buffet, and there were precisely six chairs available for people to sit down, because it was assumed everybody could stand with their glass in one hand and their plate in the other."

For anyone who is not close to Scope the reason behind Valerie's difficulties might not be apparent. However, for those of us who do know the organisation her explanation of it comes as no surprise: *"The voting members were all either local group nominees or committee members. It was the case that most local groups were made up of able-bodied people."*

In 1971 the Society suffered a profound loss when, in November, Jean Garwood died. To lose such an influential figure was bad enough, but worse was to follow. The founder had bequeathed her estate to the Society, including the property of Coombe Farm. Now, the Treasury claimed £500,000 of this, leaving the Society with £130,000. This financial injustice spurred William Burn to start a major new crusade:

"In my Chairman's Address to the AGM in October 1970, I introduced the unfair taxation treatment of charities as a nationwide project which all charities should be involved in. This soon led to the setting up of a National Advisory Group which comprised members of most leading charities, as well as the Church Commissioners, under the auspices of the National

Being There

Jack Howarth (Albert Tatlock from Coronation Street) sold autographs to help raise £50,000 for SOS. Our service in Oxford was renamed in his memory in 1972

Council for Social Services chaired by Lord Heyworth. We issued a hard-hitting report in January 1972, which received considerable publicity. In the years that followed I was often personally involved in urging the Treasury to recommend taxation policies which would assist the growth of the voluntary sector."

During his Chairmanship he also became heavily involved with SOS. *"I served on the Committee of The Stars Organisation for Spastics (SOS) between 1959 and 1973. The national Society actively encouraged the SOS not only to raise money for the main Society, but also to run its own centres, as we and they believed it was important to have centres to which the show business stars could relate to as 'their own projects'."*

Against this background it is probably not surprising that in 1972 Chiltern House was re-named Jack Howarth House after the actor who played Albert Tatlock in *Coronation Street.*

The following year the former BCWS residential home, Ponds, was re-named The Princess Marina Centre. This was in tribute to HRH Princess Marina, Patron of the Society since its amalgamation with the British Council for the Welfare of Spastics in 1963 (she had been their Patron since 1958). She will always be remembered as the Princess with the human touch. Many of her visits to schools and centres of the Society were private. On one occasion she telephoned Ponds, a home that she was very fond of, *"I have a free afternoon tomorrow and I'd love to come and visit you. May I?"* she asked.

Alex Moira saw the fruition of his dream when in June 1973 Habinteg Housing Association had officially launched a new housing integrated development for disabled people in Haringey. Habinteg had been supported in its early days by the Society but was now making its own way. Gone were the days when the Society could help other organisations as it

Being There

Alex Moira and Derek Lancaster-Gaye with Prime Minister Ted Heath at the opening of the first Habinteg development of integrated housing

struggled to keep pace with inflation. In the year 1973-74, the cost of running the Society's schools and centres shot up by 20 per cent.

The Seventies were difficult days for Bill Hargreaves, too. The 62 Clubs were becoming harder and harder to maintain. The reason? *"What happened in the end was the more able people eventually got married or got jobs or moved away, leaving behind people who the groups could care for, but hopefully care for in the right way."*

By the end of 1973 William Burn resigned as Chairman. But he was not finished with the organisation. *"I stayed on the Executive Council until '82, so that was another nine years, and I was looked upon, like Mr Moira, as a sort of advisor to the Council..."*

Changing Society

Adrian Wright, Chair of the Association of 62 Clubs, became only the second person with cp to be elected to Executive Council

Despite the financial pressures, the Society, under new Chairman Dorrien Belson, continued to innovate. In 1975, Churchtown Farm, a field study centre in Cornwall, and a conductive education unit at Ingfield Manor School in Sussex, were launched. Both introduced radically different forms of education to people with cerebral palsy. In the case of Ingfield's conductive education unit, this was later a cause of controversy as the Society was later to be accused of neglecting this form of treatment.

In 1976, the Society lost yet another of its founders, Eric Hodgson, a year before the Society's 25th anniversary. However, this decade marks the beginning of Scope involvement for another stalwart of the organisation – Pat Entwistle MBE. This is how he described it to me:

"I first got involved when I was invited to a conference in Manchester County Hall, by Nigel Smith, who was then the Regional Manager of The Spastics Society. It was a conference about transport and disabled people: the problems of disabled people travelling on public transport. That was in 1974. I didn't know about Scope then because the only contact I'd ever had was when I first started work... and I decided to ask The Spastics Society if they could help, and at the time there was a Mrs Muncaster, who was a Welfare Officer or something like that, and she found me a job at the Dunlop Rubber Company in Manchester, and that was the first-ever contact regarding the Society. That would be in 1968.

"Then, a few years later [1986], I got involved with the

Society, when we went round junior schools, talking to children about cerebral palsy, and about how it affects our lives. It was very good, and I was rather disappointed when the Society decided to knock it on the head. I thought we were getting somewhere with these children. We used to go in and show the video of 'The Land of Droog' and then we invited the children to ask questions afterwards. It was quite amazing, the questions that they did ask. Sometimes you had problems with them asking the first question: once the first question was asked, you couldn't stop them. They were really interested.

"Eventually I got involved with the regional committees of the Society. I did a turn when David Branch was coming from Liverpool from another department for six months, Peter Slark asked would I like to work for Scope for six months, and I said unfortunately I wasn't willing to give up my pension just for six months. I just didn't feel it was worth going through the hassle again, so we made the arrangement that I would travel to the office in Liverpool every day, to carry out mainly what David was doing, just for the six months, and that did work: then it finished."

Previously I described Rosamunde Browne's first involvement with Scope through the school that she and I attended. Although she went on from there to teacher training college, the latter did not end happily. The result caused the re-entry of Scope into her life:

"It wasn't until I had a breakdown three years after I became a teacher that I called on Scope – and it was still The Spastics Society then, in 1974, for advice as to what to do: could they please help me out? I had this headmistress I wasn't getting on

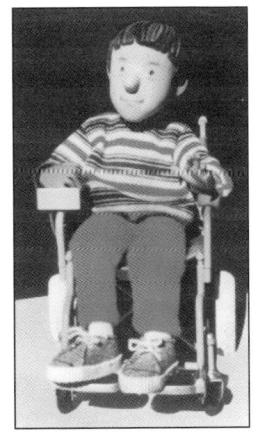

Charlie, the hero of 'Land of Droog'

with, who didn't like me and I didn't like her, and the job was getting me down, and they said, 'Resign straight away, before you're ill.' And I did. I had quite a big nervous breakdown, actually.

"They were very good and gave me the name of a place in Maidstone, Aylesford Priory, which is a Carmelite Priory, which goes back to the old medieval days, but the Carmelite Order goes back further. I was advised by Scope to go there and recuperate, and, against my will, I went there and I loved it. I take my children there now and my husband and children go there now, and we were married by a Carmelite priest. So if it wasn't for Scope, there are a lot of things that wouldn't have happened."

For John Queenborough too, the Seventies were characterised by change: "I have been involved with Scope indirectly from 1958, but directly from 1960 onwards. When I went to Glengall Road, the hostel, Scope was quite a small organisation in comparison to today's organisation. They had only offices in Park Crescent. It grew. At that point, when I first became involved it was very small, growing but very small."

Alison John first became known to the public as Alison French in a series of documentaries made by the BBC. These began in 1981 when she was a teenager. Among other things the films charted her relationship with The Spastics Society. It was not always a happy one:

"Well, I guess I must have been about two and a half years old and my Mum and Dad knew there was something wrong with me, wrong as in terms of I wasn't doing the things I was meant to be doing at the right time. Around 1966, Mum and Dad were sent to what was then called The Spastics Society, and they diagnosed me with having cerebral palsy. Then from then onwards I was under the wing of The Spastics Society.

"I think from the age of two and a half till I was 19, I had *contact with either the organisation based in Fitzroy Square; that would mean me going to visit them for assessments, or either different fieldworkers or educational workers would come and visit me in my school, home or college, to keep an eye on me to make sure I was doing the right thing at the right time. I think they thought they were enabling me to live life.*

"*I wasn't educated by Scope. When I was 10, I went for an assessment at Fitzroy Square, and it was strongly recommended that I should go to a Spastics Society school and I went to look around Wilfred Pickles, as it was called. It was a horrendous experience being showed around. There was eight beds to a dormitory, I was really frightened of the thought of being locked away with all these other spastic people. It just completely did my head in and I said, 'I'm not going.' I had so many arguments with my parents and professionals about it, I said, 'I'm not going.' I refused to be segregated away from different people with different parents. I ended up going to a mixed abilities school, where people had different impairments, which seemed to me better.*

"*First of all I went to boarding school, called Lonsdale School in Stevenage, it was a five-day boarding school. I was there from nine to 16. From 16, I went to the National Star Centre for disabled people.*"

In the 1970s Angela Smith began her school life at Delarue. Her experiences were affected by the inability of others to accommodate her ethnic identity. By the way you might recall Angela as the loving woman in a recent Government poster heralding the Disability Discrimination Act. Here's what she told me:

"*I went to a boarding school. It was difficult because I was saying goodbye to friends, and it was hard to be sent away to a totally different environment, where not many other black people were and only a handful of black children were there.*

Changing Society

Alison John

PHOTO: BBC

"It was a bit better going to Delarue School. It was better, but as you get older, you get harder. I'd already stayed about four years and I got harder, used to it, but it wasn't easier.

"I felt a sense of racial discrimination there because the houseparents they couldn't do my hair, so it got left, and they couldn't look after my skin. Black skins needs to be kept moisturised. It made me feel bad about being black."

For me too, the Seventies were a decade of change. In 1971 I had been at Oakwood Further Education College for around 18 months when I received a phone call which was to change my life drastically. To explain the consequence of this event I have to give a brief description of my parents. My mother was the activist, the parent who physically supported me most. She was and is always my champion. My father, by profession a quantity surveyor, was never physically strong and therefore left most of the physical work to Mum. But always he was supportive.

Unfortunately, he was also a hypochondriac, which was not easily accommodated by his partner, who tended towards the 'get on with it' attitude. So when Dad started to complain about stomach pains this went largely unheeded. After swallowing dozens of indigestion tablets he finally persuaded the medical profession to take notice. And so it was revealed he had gallstones, which had to be removed – a 'routine operation', we were told. I knew that he was going to have the operation but was not given any reason to be particularly concerned. The phone call I received at Oakwood was to tell me that he had died on the operating table.

I was devastated and went home to be with Mum immediately. I stayed with her until 1982. In the intervening time I applied to go to Sussex University but was told, despite the fact the University was famous for facilitating disabled people (they even supplied personal assistants), that my impairment was too severe. So then I approached Liverpool University. I wanted to study History, but found that the History building was largely inaccessible. Instead I studied Politics. My fellow students and the staff there were not always helpful and so my Mum had to support me. All my written work was done at home dictating to her. Mum even learnt to drive just so I could go to University, which was a major feat as previously she had always hated being in cars and had always left the driving to my father. For 18 months I worked my head off to the point of having a breakdown. I was totally unused to the tricks of the trade of student life and did absolutely everything I was told, never cutting corners. I couldn't take it any longer and I left. After a breathing space of 18 months I then pursued a degree at the Open University. I finally received my degree in 1982. However I was gradually

Chris Davies with his father

Changing Society

Save A Baby rally at Trafalgar Square in 1978

Dame Vera Lynn on the Save A Baby train

becoming conscious of the fact that there was no purpose to my studying, the only objective being to obtain paper qualifications. I had absolutely no idea what I would do with them. My sense of purpose came from a television programme in 1981, of which more later.

The conclusion of the Seventies was characterised by a mild attack of panic. The end of the decade saw the organisation's *Save a Baby* campaign, which with the support of the BBC *That's Life*, aimed at encouraging better pre-natal and ante-natal services which could minimise the occurrence of cerebral palsy. In 1979, the Society had a new Chair, Mrs Joyce Smith, and was to have a new Director, a high-flying businessman who was just itching to get into politics. When Tim Yeo arrived, the Society really did become more of a business. It had a record deficit of over £800,000 and had to axe services and make a number of people redundant.

One of those affected was Bill Hargreaves' department. Bill described it to me as being *"really quite appalling. My department [Recreational Services] was the first to be made redundant. They did not see it as important as the other work. In the end, one of the Directors said to me 'Bill, we know we have got rid of the wrong department.' Because I was giving people life and excitement and something to live for, especially people who would never be able to work. Give them something in life they could get hold of, be happy with and be content with. I said 'Look, I can always make cerebrally palsied people happy – even in a shed.' It was the atmosphere you created."*

But Bill was not beaten yet. He had other work to do. *"I used to run big conferences. 250 people at each. They were held at Reading University and Nottingham University and so forth. Then that led to other countries inviting me to visit them, and I visited 14 other countries, speaking in the same sort of way*

Changing Society

Tim Yeo with Joyce Smith

I had been speaking in Britain, at their expense. So a lot of my work was overseas as well." Even this was not enough. *"I was then asked to choose what I wanted to do. I said, 'Next, I want to approach the trade unions.' I even got in a handsome donation from Scargill! I did this work for only two years I then decided to retire two years early, when I was 63. I retired in 1982."*

If Chapter 2 was mainly devoted to Ian Dawson-Shepherd, and Chapter 3 to Bill Hargreaves, this chapter belongs to William Burn and Valerie Lang. To some, she may not be perceived as a radical but I guess there is some of that in all of us. I asked her about her memories of Scope and this was the highlight she chose:

"My memories include my fight and ultimate success in getting rid of what I regarded as the little, begging girls, the *dolls. I waged almost a one-woman battle against them for years and years, till Sharon Hughes backed me up and we got a sub-committee formed to discuss those, and on the committee was the inventor of these little dolls, and, poor man, you'd have thought I was murdering his children, he felt so strongly, but we got rid of them. I know some people don't like the teddy bears, but I think they are a great improvement on little begging children: so I'm very proud of having killed those off."*

You see, you don't always have to demonstrate to get things done.

Eighties

1980	1981	1983	1984
	The International Year of Disabled People.		**Spastics News** re-launched as **Disability Now**. **The Alpha Advisory Committee** of people with cerebral palsy advised Executive Council to introduce **Living Options** which promoted independent living.
	The SOS opened **Good Neighbours House. Milton Keynes Community Care Service** was also opened.	The launch of a new series of posters: **'Our worst handicap is other people's attitude.'**	

Key Dates 1980-1989

1985	1986	1988	1989	1989
Beech Tree School in Preston opened.	**First Key** scheme helped 50 residents of Kyre Park and Broadstones to move into their own homes in the community. **Douglas Shapland** replaced Joyce Smith as Chairman.	Director Sir John Cox is replaced by **Ken Young**.	**Glynn Vernon** and **Anthony Hewson** elected to Executive Council.	**Glynn Vernon** and **Anthony Hewson** elected to Executive Council.

Changing Society

Scope's patron, The Duchess of Kent, presenting a special award to Bill Hargreaves on his retirement in 1982

The Eighties, Evaluation and Rebirth

This was the decade when I became a member of staff at Park Crescent. How this happened was, at least in part, due to the work of the man who, at the beginning of the Eighties took over as Director (Chief Executive) of Scope. Today, he's better known as a politician.

Throughout its history Scope has not been known for being particularly radical. It is an irony that although it came into existence precisely because parents could not accept the *status quo* in terms of provision for people with cerebral palsy, it has still been resistant to change and prefers to maintain its own *status quo*. It then comes as somewhat of a surprise that the person who introduced a new radicalism into the organisation is a Conservative. But that's exactly what Tim Yeo did.

This is how he came to be in the job:

"I first became involved when I read an advertisement for the post, as it was called then, of 'Director' of The Spastics Society. This was in 1980, and I was interested in this job, and therefore spent several weeks carrying out quite detailed research about

the organisation: what its activities were; who were the people who were involved in it already, and what this job might actually entail. I was aware of its existence, because it was already quite a high-profile organisation, but I didn't know a huge amount about it, and that's why I spent quite a lot of time doing the research.

"I didn't know a huge amount about cerebral palsy either: probably just what I like to think of as an intelligent layman's interest in the subject. I was already very interested in disability issues, particularly because of a very, very close friend, who was a solicitor in the City, who was wheelchair-bound as a result of having suffered from polio when he was a child, and I was very aware as a result of my friendship with him of the problems of access, which were even worse than they are today, and the effective discrimination which exists in many fields of employment. It wasn't my only involvement, but it was the relationship, which had made me most aware of some of the issues confronting both individual people with disabilities and some of the broader policy considerations. I had other experiences, partly through my own political interests, partly through some of the voluntary work I did at that time."

He has a very clear memory of the organisation, as it was when he joined:

"It was an organisation which I think had completed its first phase of existence; a rather successful phase, in terms of enormous expansion from a very small beginning. I think it had sort of exhausted that phase. It was at a transitional period really. It needed to have a public profile, which was a bit sharper. I think it was at a transitional stage in terms of the influence of the parents, the parental generation that had founded the organisation. It was ready to be handed over to allow disabled people themselves to play a much bigger role in the *management of the organisation, both as volunteers and as staff. I think it was at a transitional phase in terms of its financial position too: after its huge expansion in the Sixties, the finances when I became Director were actually not very good. We had a very substantial deficit, I remember."*

When asked about his achievements as Director, he is equally clear: *"I would like to think that it changed, firstly, in being recognised much more widely as an organisation which had views which should be listened to: that it started to campaign in a more aggressive way, on a range of issues which are of direct relevance, whether they are ranged across the fields of employment, of disability rights, of taxation, of benefits and so on – quite a broad range. Secondly, I think that the organisation developed a reputation for being the most efficient in its field: that it was seen to be an organisation which had a clear set of aims, which delivered those aims, which was run well, which expected a lot from the people who worked for it, used its resources in a very efficient sort of way.*

"Thirdly, I think the organisation changed in that disabled people started to play a bigger role: not perhaps as big as has subsequently been achieved, but certainly a bigger role by the time I left from when I'd arrived, in senior positions in the management of the organisation and on the voluntary side – people who set the policy at Executive Council level and through the other committees. Fourthly, I think the financial position was very greatly improved as well. The organisation was much stronger financially when I left than when I'd arrived. The fundraising had increased significantly.

"So, I'd like to think it was a better organisation. It was certainly a better known one. I'd like to think it was a better run organisation and an organisation, which delivered, not just services, but also on a whole range of aims, both with, by,

through, on behalf of, people with cerebral palsy."

Just in case you missed it, let me emphasise that he said that he gave a bigger role in management to people with cerebral palsy. That is radical. How did he do it? This is how he explains it:

"One of the first things I did was to re-focus a group of advisors, who we called 'The Consumers' Group', which gave them not only direct access to me, but we used to meet regularly in my office at Park Crescent, and I don't think this had been done in quite that way before. I'd like to think that there was a period when a very large proportion of the Society's policies was actually tested with the Consumers' Group, as well as being discussed at The Executive Council and through the other committees. The Chairman of this group became quite a close friend of mine, Ron Gurver, and I worked closely with him during this period.

"We also made a more deliberate attempt to appoint people with disabilities to key jobs within the organisation. I have to say I was quite surprised when I started working for the organisation at how relatively few of the senior management positions were held by people with disabilities. There was a reasonable representation on the committees... I think that those were aims that were in my mind. I daresay that we didn't fulfil them as much as we should have done, but at least they were there in my mind. I think that on the Council during most of the time that I was there, we had three people, and again it struck me that, even during my time, it was still a very parent-dominated organisation. It was founded by parents, so it was natural that they should be influential at the start, but I think, in the way that parents always find difficult, they weren't letting go of it, and as it happens, I think parents who've got a disabled child in the family find it particularly hard to allow the normal process of growing up to take place."

Evaluation and Rebirth

That is not all he achieved, nor was it all that was radical.

"*Another of the tasks that faced us in the early Eighties was to bring some of those services up to date: that Scope had become very much involved in providing residential care in large country houses, that it was very committed to special education in schools, and one of the changes I made which I was particularly proud of was that I started an organisation called 'The Centre for Studies on Integration in Education', which was a very strong campaigning body, designed to try and produce more integrated education.*

"*We had some very powerful advertising, which was designed to expose the degree of discrimination which took place. I remember that one of the advertisements we produced was a picture of someone backing their car into a space that was reserved for disabled people. The caption was 'Is this the only time that you put yourself in the position of a disabled person?' We had a series of fairly hard-hitting advertisements, which were run for us by Benton & Bowles, and quite controversial. The Executive Council was not at all happy about this campaign, but the staff were determined to run it, and it did make a big impact, and I think that it showed the organisation in a very positive light.*"

This was not an isolated example of resistance from traditional thinkers.

"*I found it difficult to achieve change in one respect: because of the structure, that the ultimate policy is set by the Executive Council, and therefore, if they don't wish to go along with a particular idea, in the end it's almost impossible for anyone else, even the most senior of staff, to put it into practice. Where I found that there was a lot of help was amongst some of the staff.*

"*I was lucky that I was able to recruit quite a lot of the staff whilst I was there: a lot of the senior jobs became vacant, and*

Changing Society

so we had, I think, for a time a very enthusiastic group of staff, many of whom had quite radical ideas about what they wanted to do, and there was no resistance from them at all. I think they were very supportive of the changes, but there was I have to say, some resistance – I don't want to stigmatise the Executive Council because they are volunteers and a lot of them have been extraordinarily dedicated in what they've done and Scope wouldn't exist if it hadn't been for them over the years, but nevertheless, I feel that they were resistant to change in a way which many staff members were not resistant to change."

I asked him about the experiences he had during his time as Director: *"I remember early on, quite soon after I'd joined the organisation, there was going to be a debate in Parliament about the issue of intensive care for babies: neo-natal intensive care, and we, as an organisation, had very strong views about this, naturally, and I remember my surprise that when we expressed these views, the then Minister of Health, a chap called Gerry Vaughan, who was Minister of Health in about 1980, actually leapt in his car and came round to Park Crescent, to hear what I had to say. I was impressed by this. My expectation was, on the whole, that if you wanted to get Ministers to listen to your views you had to knock on their door, and, if you were lucky, you got about 10 minutes of their time. He was an example, I thought, of how this organisation already carried considerable weight, in terms of its campaigning ability.*

"I remember, again early on, one of the successes that I had was getting the Blue Peter Appeal, in the winter of 1981, just before the start of the International Year of Disabled People. The Blue Peter Appeal was on behalf of IYDP, and it was administered by us. I remember volunteering to man the telephones one weekend, and we had to keep the telephones going all during the weekend, and the absolutely delightful

Evaluation and Rebirth

Tim Yeo and Joyce Smith greet Indira Gandhi on her visit to Fitzroy Square in 1982

PHOTO: MARGARET MURRAY

support of the young audience of 'Blue Peter', who raised money through a series of bring and buy sales, and the lovely descriptions that quite small children were very keen to give over the telephone to the organisation for which they were raising money, of the events of their bring and buy sales.

"*I remember the occasion when we entertained Indira Gandhi at Fitzroy [Square] – we showed her round when she was on a visit to London; I think this was in 1982. As Prime Minister of what was then the largest democracy in the world, we had visited her in India the year before, when a group of us were out there, working with The Spastics Society of India, as it was called. When she came back, she came round to see the assessment work we were doing at Fitzroy, and I've got a nice photograph of her on that visit. But what struck me on that visit was, relatively speaking, the lack of media interest, compared with when we'd had Nancy Reagan the year before. Nancy*

Changing Society

Reagan came to London for the Prince of Wales' wedding, in July 1981, and, through the US Embassy, I invited her to come round (this was really, I have to say, a publicity exercise for the organisation). She also came to Fitzroy. We had more TV cameras at Fitzroy that day than I've ever seen in any voluntary organisation. We had all the main US TV channels; we had all the British channels and most of the European channels. We had to allocate one room to each of these TV stations, so they could film her, mostly meeting youngsters, but also talking to staff at Fitzroy.

"*We had a literary award, which anyone with cerebral palsy could enter. There were different categories for poems, for short stories, and there were age groups; a section for children and a section for adults, and I remember we always used to get an author to present the awards, and one year we invited Jeffrey Archer, of all people, to present the awards, and it was the first time I really saw Jeffrey Archer in a tremendously favourable light. He came into this room, and you will know how even really quite experienced people are phased if they're in a roomfull of people, quite often severely handicapped people: they don't quite know how to react, they don't quite know how to behave. He was totally natural; he was totally normal. I could see people were responding to him with great enthusiasm, because he was saying, 'Well done! You've come second! Now next year I want you to come first!' and so on. It was an entirely positive response that he had managed to achieve, and it was interesting, seeing someone well-known in a completely new light, as a result of their enthusiasm.*"

Tim Yeo did not entirely disappear from Scope in 1983.

"*After I'd stopped being Director at the end of December 1983, I continued to be involved in a number of ways, most notably through my political work. I did serve rather briefly –*

Evaluation and Rebirth

I think for two years – on the Executive Council as well, from 1984 to 1986."

It was the advertising campaign mentioned by Tim Yeo which, indirectly, brought me to Park Crescent. However by the time it happened, my life had changed totally.

In 1981 an hour watching TV was the catalyst for a total change in direction in my life.

Jeffrey Archer with John Cox at the launch of 'Write Angles' in October 1984 PHOTO: SIDNEY HARRIS

The United Nations declared 1981 The International Year of Disabled People. At least that is what I prefer to call it. If one was being pedantic, one might want to stick to the American original title, which had 'Persons' instead of 'People'. Or, if you can remember the year, you might remember the media chose to call it 'International Year of the Disabled' and I don't recall that much lasting good came from this year but it did mean a significant rise in the amount of television programmes on disability. Many of these were well-meaning, but nevertheless highly medically-orientated, documentaries. There was a great deal of patronising material, hardly any of it was from the perspective of disabled people themselves.

I remember just three. The first was in the BBC2 *Man Alive* series of documentaries called *Extra Ordinary People*. It featured three people just living their lives. One of these, Steve Burton, had been at Delarue School with me and has now become a lawyer. It also included a young teenager, Alison French. She made such an impression that, within the same year, she would have a documentary all to herself.

The second memorable programme, also on BBC2, was within

the scientific series *Horizon*. This was a drama documentary about a man called Joey Deacon. Joey has lived most of his life in an institution, educating himself and now beginning to live independently. Another disabled person, Joey's best friend, wrote down Joey's life story, which then became a book. The film was memorable not simply because of its content, but also because for the flashback sequences, the leading characters were played by disabled actors (mostly). It was this documentary which was used as a basis for the *Blue Peter* appeal that year.

These programmes I remember clearly but they did not change my life. The one that did so, was shown in November 1990 on ITV. It was made by a production team, which was responsible for a regular disability programme *Link*. In the North West where I lived, we had never seen this programme because Granada was one of only two companies that did not show *Link* at all. So I was totally unprepared for the programme about disability politics, presented by a disabled person. *We Won't Go Away* was broadcast by the whole network and showed how disabled people in America had successfully fought for civil rights. It was presented by Rosalie Wilkins, a wheelchair-user. The effect on me was devastating. All my life I have been fascinated by TV, but never thought that I could be a part of it. But I saw Rosalie do it, so why couldn't I? Not only did I see what I wanted to do; I also saw why I wanted to do it. I was certain that I wanted to use television to influence society towards equality.

So I did the only thing I could. I wrote a script based on a very commonplace understanding of television techniques and sent it the BBC Community Programme Unit. At that time they made *Open Door*, a series of programmes originated and controlled by the public made with the assistance of BBC professionals. Amazingly I was accepted and from the end of January 1982

Evaluation and Rebirth

I produced and presented *Attitudes: The Second Handicap*. Originally it was 20 minutes then it was extended to 50 minutes. Suddenly people had heard of me. By the end of that year I was negotiating with Channel 4 to make programmes with a production company I initiated. The BBC helped me to go to New York to promote *Attitudes* at an International Disability Film Festival. Ironically, my programme tied with *We Won't Go Away*.

Then I received a phone call from the Head of Publicity at Park Crescent asking me whether I would consider being a subject in one of the posters of which Tim Yeo is so proud. That was the start of a friendship, which was to help me start my independent living.

The poster with me never happened, but I kept in contact with the publicity department and they were well aware of my outrage at the choice of successor to Tim Yeo.

I was never totally convinced that a businessman was a particularly good choice to be in charge of a disability charity, but the choice of an ex-Vice Admiral of the Fleet seemed totally wrong. I was encouraged to put my thoughts to paper and they were printed. To my amazement he invited me to lunch and I found myself liking him. Indeed, eventually and for three and half years I worked with him in the publicity department at Park Crescent.

I was not around when Sir John Cox left the Society, so when we met for the interview for this book it was somewhat of a reunion. It was also the first time he'd been near Scope since his departure. Even though I thought I knew him quite well, much of what he had done was new to me. For example how he came to be Director. He told me:

"*I had decided to leave the Royal Navy and I left it early, as a Vice Admiral. I was always interested in disability. I opened the paper and saw there was a vacancy for a Chief Executive in The Spastics Society, so I applied.*"

Changing Society

Sir John Cox and Brian Rix campaigning on community care PHOTO: VIC FOWLER

As I was unaware of any prior interest in disability, I asked him about this. He explained:

"As a young lieutenant... I had to prepare [a Governor's] visit, both to a long-stay hospital and to a children's home with severely disabled children – severely – and I found myself wanting: I found I couldn't take it. I went away after the visit and said to my Governor, 'Please, I've got to go away and talk to myself.' And I went away and talked to myself for about a week.

"From that moment onwards, I slowly learnt to acknowledge that – it was just like being in the navy in different ships: different cap tallies, different persons, different ways, and that's how I became interested; and from then onwards, in every ship I was in, I made certain that sailors were professionals at sea and citizens in harbour. In harbour they were dealing with children, with adults, in long-stay hospitals, in residential homes, and so

you can say from the time I was a lieutenant I was involved. My mother-in-law was severely disabled in her latter years, so I was more than personally involved."

Naturally, he prepared himself before applying and formed a distinct impression of the organisation.

"I did a lot of research before I even put my name forward, and my research made me full of respect for the people who started The Spastics Society; the ones who had children and started it with nothing. The Government did nothing for them and I thought they were fantastic, and I was very happy to be involved with such a society. When I came, it was a society with about 2,900 personnel and with an annual turnover of, I think, £29 million.

"I think like any great society or charity who's come from nothing to £30 million in thirty-odd years, and producing schools, residential centres etc. etc., there comes a time when it actually needs to look at itself and see whether its footprints are going in the right direction, or whether they should change. When I arrived, I found that there was, despite the amount of money, a deficit, and I didn't see any plan forward, either short- or long-term – or even objectives, and I felt this was something that needed to be looked at: but, having said that, I was very impressed with the staff that I was dealing with. I made it my job to go round as many of the establishments in the regions as I could, as fast as I could."

What, I asked, did he find when he first arrived?

"Within, I think, the first 18 months, as I'd found that there was no plan forward, I did suggest that there should be a real look at the work of The Spastics Society and at whether the staff were the right professionals in the right jobs, or whether there should be a difference. For instance, are residential homes correct in this day and age? I didn't think they probably were *for an awful lot, and as we know, schools were changing. As a result of which, we had a two-day 'talk-in' at Castle Priory. I invited two of the Council: Hildreth and Berry, to see fair play. They didn't actually believe in what I was doing until afterwards, when they said they were very happy with what had come out: looking at – how shall I put it? – the debit and credit side of The Spastics Society and where perhaps it might change.*

"That took a long time: in fact, it took an awful long time to get as much money in as was going out. I don't think I achieved that properly [until], I think, Year 3. Certainly in Year 4 I was well in the black. But this was something which had to be addressed very, very soon."

Like his predecessor, John Cox has clear memories of his time at Scope.

"I remember people in the main. People, whether one's talking about those with very, very severe disabilities, which the school in Preston [Beech Tree] and the one just north of London [Meldreth] – they did so well: in other words, the ones with children who'd come from long-stay hospitals. I was incredibly impressed with the standard of staff. I was impressed with the friendliness of those with cerebral palsy and those who were members of the regions, the groups, and also with the staff itself. I think my over-riding, overwhelming feeling is people, people, people.

"There are so many stories. One thing I think would always say to anyone who's becoming Chief Executive of The Spastics Society or Scope is, 'Be very careful if you accept an invitation to a disco with people in a wheelchair, because I've never had so many broken toes in 25 years of rugby.'"

While I was working at Park Crescent, the Marketing Department instigated a market research survey on the value of the name. Not surprisingly, therefore John Cox told me of another memory:

"I remember one of the very first things I was disappointed in – I don't know how else to put it – were the words 'Spastics Society'. I tried to encourage the Council to see whether the name of the society could reflect the modern look, as the word 'spastic' was in fact outlawed in America, Canada and Australia."

At this stage, the argument was not yet won. The survey proved to be inconclusive and there was still too much pressure from an older generation of parents and people with cerebral palsy to retain the old name.

During my time in the PR department I played an active part in the production of two videos, including *Land of Droog*, an animation video for children. After three and a half years I moved on but there was one part of my work which has had a lasting effect. As a move intended to encourage those who disliked anything to do with the current name of the organisation, the PR department wanted to revamp its magazine, still called *Spastics News*. I was asked to deliver a list of possible names for the new publication. On that list was *Disability Now*. I will never know whether the eventual choice was made from my list or not, but I feel proud that I played a part.

Tim Yeo and John Cox are new contributors to this story. Time now to catch up with the story of two people who have already appeared.

For Alex Moira, the Eighties were the time when he bowed out of Scope. He described the end of his Scope career like this:

"When I left in about 1981 or '2, it had 64, I think, projects of one kind built and running, and a similar number (I'm not exactly sure of the precise number) of group services, a few of which were residential, like Newcastle, for instance: but most of which were day services of one kind or another, and The Spastics Society was then thought to be the largest charity

Changing Society

in the country. When I left in '81 or so, I left completely, merely because I wanted to do some other things and hadn't time to do both, and so I have not kept in touch at all with the development of Scope, and as far as the time that I was concerned with it, we had more or less got to the size which I think any charity cannot go beyond."

For Andrew Berry it was a time for becoming extremely involved. This is Andrew's explanation of his deepening links with Scope:

"I first became involved when I moved to Milton Keynes, with a local group; although I had actually done a couple of sponsored walks for Scope: various one-off things, things I did with various school friends; but then I got involved in about 1982/1983 with the local group in Milton Keynes. At the time I was going out with a girl who happened to be the daughter of the secretary of the local group, and she persuaded me that it would be a good idea to get involved. I suppose, right from the start, I always knew that I'd get more involved, and in 1985, I think it was, I applied to become a member of the Executive Council, and, much to my amazement, I was elected the first time, and I've been on the Council ever since. I've done a number of things. I've been Vice Chairman for a year: I've been Chairman of Marketing, when we had a Marketing Committee: a number of things."

Ken Young, who had been involved in local government, followed John Cox as Chief Executive. By now, Mrs Joyce Smith was the Chair, but waiting in the wings were two people who were going to, between them, instigate the most profound change yet in the organisation.

One of these has already been introduced. Glynn Vernon, who went to school with me, is a plain-speaking Yorkshireman and a radical. For a while, he had been distanced from the organisation but then things changed. He told me:

Evaluation and Rebirth

Andrew Berry completes an abseil with Richard Brewster, Scope's current Chief Executive

"I came back to change things. I came back because, by that time, I'd become a user again, and I saw how users were treated by The Spastics Society. I won't use the word 'Scope' in this context, because it wasn't 'Scope': it was The Spastics Society. What happened was, I was part of the service, which was the Neath professional workshop, and somebody came down from London and said 'We're going to close this service next week.' No consultation, no preparation, just that. That made me very, very angry and I don't think I thought, 'Can I change The Spastics Society', I thought, 'I'm going to bloody change it!' I knew it wasn't going to be easy. I think if I went back 10 years now, and not knowing people like Anthony Hewson were going to be around, I don't think I would have attempted it. But luckily, I wasn't the only person who thought, 'I want to change the Society.'"

Changing Society

But Anthony Hewson was around. Glynn and Anthony learned from each other and gave each other support. I know Anthony quite well now and I suspect there wasn't much radical about him initially. In the first place, he was a businessman working in the motoring industry. And then his son came on to the scene. The birth of Toby changed everything:

"Toby appeared in this world. That was 18 years ago now. I suppose the first contact I had with The Spastics Society at that time was about four weeks after he was diagnosed with cerebral palsy, which was 11 months after he'd been born. My mother phoned The Spastics Society and had this rather odd conversation about wanting to become a member, but you'll remember at that time you couldn't become a member. However, they sent her an action pack and off we went, so that was my first contact with The Spastics Society at that time. I think the first major involvement was when he went to Ingfield Manor School, when he was 18 months old. We carried him through the door, as they say. Then we started (over some five/six years) to be interested in The Spastics Society and its work and things grew from there.

"We discovered he had cerebral palsy 11 months after he was born. The paediatrician came to the house and we discovered some years later, not at that time, that my mother and one of his godparents had become concerned about his 'development': they thought there was something amiss and suggested we ought to have him looked at, so the paediatrician came to the house the day after New Year's Day. It's an odd little memory, but perhaps worthy of record that when he said to me, 'Your son has cerebral palsy', I looked at him and said 'And what tablets do you prescribe for that?'

"I suppose it's interesting to think about that and then the name change and everything that followed, because he said,

Evaluation and Rebirth

Glynn Vernon with Scope's president, the Duke of Westminster

'No, I don't think you quite understand Mr Hewson. It means he will be a spastic', and of course immediately the vision of what I was to learn years later, the vision of the child in the wheelchair, the image that had been created when The Spastics Society had been formed, really all came quickly into view."

That's how it started and it might have stopped there but for his wife Elizabeth who contrived to bring her husband closer to the organisation.

"Elizabeth went up there [Scope's Ingfield Manor School in West Sussex] with increasing frequency for the first year: first of all it was just for the afternoon, and then for two or three afternoons: the usual process, and then she stopped going, because they don't want parents hanging around schools. I think it was when Toby was about five or six, I remember Elizabeth came back from a function at the school that I hadn't been able to get to because I'd been away on business and she said, 'There's quite a lot of trouble up there. People want to leave and things. You ought to come along and meet them.'

"I remember saying, 'That's the last thing I want to do, as actually they're perfectly capable of running their own business, a bloody big organisation like that. Leave them alone.' And about two months later she invited me to a pub, which was quite unusual mid-week, and I went along to meet two of the other parents whose children had started with Toby, ostensibly, except half the staff of Ingfield were in the pub as well, so I suppose I realised that we were in the snare at this point.

"All these very committed people decided to unburden themselves at great length about their problems, which really amounted to the fact that The Spastics Society really couldn't give a toss about what they were doing and had forgotten them, or at least, that was their perception. They were very fed up and people were leaving. I was appalled by it, frankly, because it smacked of bad management, nothing to do with schools or charities, just poor person management if you like."

From then he was 'in the snare':

"So we wrote a paper called The Way Forward... What this attempted to do was to tell the Executive Council that they were about to make a grave error of judgement and could they please get their bloody act together? I remember we went to see Joyce Smith on a Sunday evening. The three people who went will tell you to this minute what it was like. It was like going to visit God. We had to drive down to Salisbury and there she sat – like a queen – conducting whatever ceremony was going on. We were ushered into her presence – this is the Chairman of The Spastics Society – and we told her our story and I always remember her at the end grabbing the telephone alongside her and dialling Freddie Green's number and I remember thinking 'I'm bloody glad I'm not Freddie Green.' Fortunately for Freddie, he was out, so she couldn't get hold of him: if she had have done, I think he'd have been lying in pieces on the floor.

"So we saw her and, to be fair, she gave us a hearing in front of the Council – not actually a full Council, a committee of Council, and we made a presentation and then we were invited to our first AGM.

"That's a wonderful experience, isn't it? It was in that huge Imperial College: do you remember where the Council used to sit, on a huge stage, so high up you needed binoculars to see them… I remember this guy – quite a well-known man in The Spastics Society at that time – standing up and saying he was very worried, very concerned, that children with cerebral palsy at Ingfield Manor were learning Conductive Education, because they may develop traits towards communism, since it had been developed in an Eastern bloc country.

"Elizabeth, who was sitting alongside me with other friends – there was a brass rail in front, and she said she watched my knuckles go white and I put my hand up and caught the Chair's eye – Joyce, in her last AGM – and she called me to speak, which was really quite an honour from Joyce. I said I had not intended to speak at this meeting but I wanted to reassure people that my son, who was eight years old and who had been receiving Conductive Education since the age of 18 months, had not to my certain knowledge, yet developed any Marxist

Changing Society

Doug Shapland (in the centre) was responsible, with Anthony Hewson (far left), for sending 12 trainees to the Petö Centre in Budapest in 1990 to learn the principles of Conductive Education

tendencies. It got quite a laugh. But it was misinformation that I was a bit unhappy about."

Anthony became the authority on Conductive Education, the system of learning developed in Budapest to help children with motor impairments learn how to perform everyday tasks:

"After that, Doug Shapland was elected and he invited me to go with him to Hungary, because of course the relationship with Hungary was in tatters... The whole thing was a mess. We had parents picketing Park Crescent, do you remember? I'd rather not remember it. Anyway, he asked me to accompany him on every trip he made and we worked with Maria Hari [of the Petö Institute] to repair things. It was very, very hard work."

Doug Shapland encouraged Anthony to stand for Executive Council in November 1989. He was elected first time.

Evaluation and Rebirth

Within six weeks, Doug Shapland was dead and suddenly Anthony Hewson found himself touted by Council colleagues as his replacement. He must have had few doubts about the challenge ahead:

"When I first went on the Council, within the first six months, I knew the organisation was out of control. I went to a meeting of the Finance Committee… It was out of control financially. It was out of control in management terms. We fired the Chief Executive and the Finance Director within the first 18 months. It was hopelessly out of control.

"It was out of control in terms of its most senior levels of management and their relations with the Council. Of course, it didn't have a membership other than local groups, but it certainly wasn't listening to people with cerebral palsy, and, in my view, it didn't seem to be representing anybody's interests but its own.

"I think it was an unhappy organisation. There are lots of symptoms of that. If you went to a regional committee meeting, they were normally at war, weren't they? Everybody arrived prepared for battle. There was an extraordinary culture that prevailed: it was one of staff against trustees or staff against volunteers, and people with disabilities in the middle of it… or nowhere."

This was precisely what Anthony changed. The place of disabled people was about to be moved from the margins. 'The Spastics Society' was giving way to 'Scope' and the father of the change was Anthony Hewson – with a little push from Glynn Vernon.

Nineties

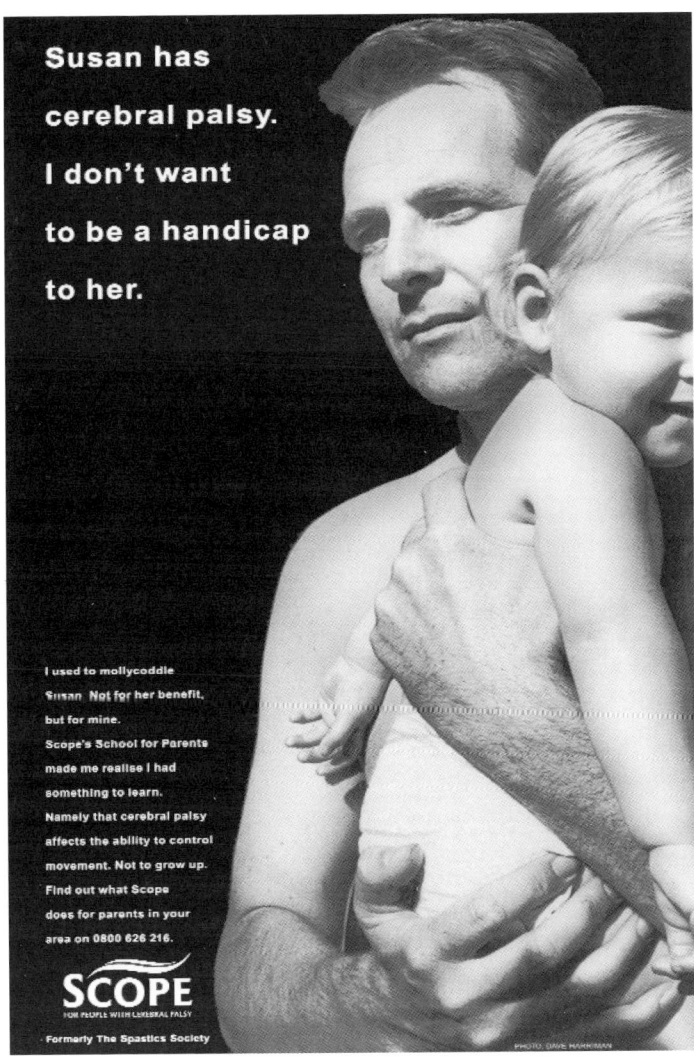

1990	1991	1992	1994
	The 200th Spastics Society shop opened.		The Spastics Society became **Scope**.
Fast-Track, a development programme for disabled graduates, and the **Cerebral Palsy Helpline** launched.		**The Petö Centre** and the **Dame Vera Lynn School for Parents** opened. The **Polls Apart** survey showed that 88% of polling stations were inaccessible.	

Key Dates 1990-1999

1996	1997	1998	1998
	Hawksworth School and the wheelchair factory **Newton Products** closed. Chair Anthony Hewson was replaced by Chairman **Jim Hoskisson**.		Scope announced its new aim that disabled people achieve equality.
Scope launched an individual **membership** scheme.		Scope's Executive Council had a majority of disabled people.	

Changing Society

Claire Rayner at the launch of the CP Helpline in 1990

The Nineties: Changing for the 21st Century

The last decade of the 20th century mainly, in terms of this organisation, was the province of Chairman Anthony Hewson. This is how he believes the organisation had evolved:

"We had these three or four phases: we had the start of it and the huge enthusiasm, and by any standards, a huge success, which, interestingly enough, with the benefit of hindsight, actually built up a very large number of problems that we had to sort out. If you spend money like a drunken sailor, you're likely to remain a bit hit-and-miss for quite a time, and that's what [it] did. The Spastics Society was very, very wealthy. I've read minutes of AGM's where the parents were standing up and really giving the Council hell for not spending it. I can't remember AGM's like that because the money had gone when I arrived, but that's what happened: tremendous pressures to spend the money, to create the services, and I think that was very good.

"Then we go into the period of what I call bureaucracy: endless management and trustees. The third phase is what I call the 'falling-off-the-edge' phase, when things really hit rock

Changing Society

Anthony Hewson signs the historic agreement with Dr Hari of the Petö Institute in 1992
PHOTO: ANNA TULLY

bottom and nobody will do anything to sort it out and it just endlessly goes round in circles.

"The fourth phase is the shake-up: there are little shake-ups across the whole period. I think when we embarked on the process of name-change we examined very carefully what the organisation was about and what it stood for, or didn't. We looked into its innermost workings with more magnification than had ever been done before and, of course, what we saw was something that we didn't like very much. It was very uncomfortable and what we found was we had an organisation that didn't represent the interests of the people it had been born to serve."

I asked him to describe his memories of that period: "I remember going to my first council meeting at Castle Priory and going into Coombe Farm, which was being closed at that time. I can remember people weeping whilst I was there and I was very angry about that. Even during the closure of a unit we didn't seem to get our message across. Closing somebody's home is bound to be an emotional issue. We were messing people's lives about. I sensed the damp hand of bureaucracy, the heavy hand of bureaucracy all over this. That was my early outstanding memory.

"Of course, I have an outstanding memory about Ingfield: a place of such immense quality and care and love: a better school you could not have found. It was extraordinary, the commitment of the people, and openness to listen.

Changing for the 21st Century

"*I remember after a few meetings, gathering enough courage, because that's what you needed in those days – most people didn't speak for the first year – I remember quietly saying, 'I wonder if we could all remember why we're here? We are here for people with cerebral palsy, not because we like running charities.'*

"*Another outstanding memory was the name change and the process. [The EGM] was an extraordinary day. Maybe I have a slightly different memory of it to a lot of people, because I was the apparent leader of this lot. We had worked our way through four years of preparation, and in front of me was a sea of wheelchairs, none of whom could vote. I remember thinking to myself, what the hell was I going to do if the vote didn't go the right way? I thought they'd probably wheel forward and lynch me.*"

The Duke of Westminster celebrates the Society's 40th anniversary with Esther Rantzen
PHOTO: MICHELLE SMITH

I, too, remember this occasion. I was present at both meetings that decided the issue of the name. The tension was quite extraordinary. On one hand, you had staff and Council members who were heavily in favour of change, but who remained unsure right to the end about how this decision would go. On the other, you had the delegates who had it within their power to deny the possibility of change. At that point in the history of Scope there was no membership of the organisation. Local groups chose their own representatives and delegates. Most local groups had few or no disabled people on their management committees.

Changing Society

Anthony Hewson lobbying parliament for better educational opportunities for disabled children in 1993

Therefore there were hardly any delegates who were disabled people. At both meetings there were lots of disabled people, but they were observers and could only watch while other people made the decisions that affected them. Delegates must have known how deeply those who could not vote felt about the issue.

The choice of possible names was not fantastic. However, quite by accident, I think I may have found the person who first offered the option of the name that was chosen. Andrew Berry told me:

"We had a series of meetings around the country when we were changing the name, in order to bring everybody along with it. I attended most of those meetings, and one of the processes that we went through was brainstorming. At one of the meetings we were talking about the idea of what Scope is really all about. Somebody came up with the idea of range;

Changing for the 21st Century

My Right! was the first fundraising campaign to focus on the rights of people with cerebral palsy

a wide range of activities; a wide range of objectives and so on. I suddenly said in the meeting 'Well, that's about scope', and about three months later, the staff had sort of mangled all the information up and 'Scope' was the name to be selected. So I'm not saying I'm responsible, but I am saying that perhaps I had a significant contribution."

Market research recommended 'Scope' from a shortlist of options. My personal opinion is that this had the most potential – much more so than any others on the list (Cerebral Palsy Society, Action Cerebral Palsy, Capability and Action Disability). However, it is far from perfect, not least because it is not self-explanatory. Although the full title is, I think, 'Scope for people with cerebral palsy' (that's what it says on the letterheads), which is self-explanatory, if the first word is the only one that gets used, then the title begs too many questions. But, in

Changing Society

different ways, other titles available would have had difficulties attached to them.

Many people in this book have an opinion about the change of name, and not all are in favour. Before I go on to these, let's just finish the story about the historic meeting when the change was made. The one aspect I remember most clearly is the intangible sense of relief when the decision to change was taken. Anthony Hewson was sure that the process that led to the decision was the appropriate one. This is how he saw it from the platform:

"I think we were right to be cautious, because a 75 per cent majority was necessary. The reality was that although we won it by many, many votes, the overall margin was 79.4 and 80.2: that's not a huge number of people in a meeting of that size, so I think we were right to be careful."

And afterwards...

"It was initially a sense of relief. I did a lot of crying afterwards. It was a big success for The Spastics Society, but it was a big personal success as well."

There was, at this meeting, a defining moment. It was when someone made a very eloquent speech in favour of change. He was not the only person who spoke from this point of view, but he was the person who swung opinion towards change. He did so because of who he was. Everybody knew how he always defined himself as 'spastic'. If he could see the sense behind the change, then there wasn't much reason not to do it. By now, it should come as no surprise to learn that it was Bill Hargreaves. That defining moment was recorded on video and played again at the 2000 AGM as part of the tribute to Bill. Not surprisingly, in his interview with me he remembered that day:

"When they changed the name to Scope, I spoke up for it, as you probably know. Somebody had to speak as I did, and do you know why?

Changing for the 21st Century

As Spastics Society signage is dismantled, William Hague witnesses the unfurling of the Scope flag at St Thomas's hospital in 1994 (overleaf)

SCOPE

OPLE WITH CEREBRAL PALSY

The Spastics Society

Changing Society

Ben Elton helps to publicise the name-change and Scope shops get a face-lift.
Bill Hargreaves spoke in favour of changing the Society's name to Scope

"You had to get, in the end, an amalgamation of the old and the new, and I tried to achieve that. To see that an old boy is saying, 'God bless, do it.'"

Up to this point, most of the contributors have been quite positive about Scope. However, this is not to say that none of the people I interviewed were not at all critical. Those who were critical doubted whether their views would eventually be included, either because Scope couldn't take criticism or because I personally did not agree with the views being expressed. This is where I prove this wrong.

Rosamund Browne went to the same school as I did and has had occasional dealings with Scope. These have led to her assisting the Stars Organisation for Scope. When I asked her how this happened, her answer spilled over into these views she has about the name of the organisation. It may surprise you, as it did me.

"I know where our local Scope headquarters is; it's in Portsmouth. I live in Pennington, which is New Forest area, and I'd been in touch with what they call 'the social worker' Nigel Marsh once or twice. He wanted to see how I was doing as a married person, running a house and so we said 'Hi' to each other and he left, and I said 'If I need anything I'll ring you', and then in 1997, somebody phoned me out of the blue and said 'Do you fancy performing at the Queen Elizabeth Hall?' and I said, 'I'm sorry, come again?' I said 'Yes, I would really, really love to. Excuse me, what made you choose me?' and she said, 'Well, this is by way of an audition, this phone call a) you're one of the few I can understand straight away. I wanted to see (sic) what you sounded like, and b), what caught my attention was that you still refer to yourself as a spastic. You don't refer to yourself as having cerebral palsy.' I said, 'Because I've always been a spastic. I grew up with the word. School kids

Changing Society

Bob Waring MP at the launch of Disabled In Britain 1994
PHOTO: STEVE HICKEY

used to come up to me and say 'Miss, he's a spastic' and I used to have to explain that 'He's not a spastic, but I am.' It was a good conversation-opener. Now they've changed it to cerebral palsy, and I can't be doing with it.

"I don't like political correctness at all. I can't see anything wrong with the word 'spastic': I was brought up with the word 'spastic'. It's a wonderful conversation-opener. I think 'cerebral palsy' is a dreadful expression. It reminds me of the Bible and begging. And 'spastic'. OK, it was bandied around to mean 'dim' or 'thick' or 'mental', but as soon as anybody mentioned that word in my hearing, I was able to leap in and explain it, thereby spreading the gospel that way. Now they've called it 'Scope' and nobody knows what the hell they're on about. I don't know what it means. Nobody else knows what it means. The [London headquarters] building's better: you can get into the building all right, but you can't get round the name. Scope doesn't even stand for anything, does it? It's too airy-fairy and too nice. It doesn't call a spade a spade.

"I think 'spastic' is a wonderful word. It's great, but then, as I say, when you've had a class-full of kids... I walked into a room one day and one of them whispered to the other, 'Stand up you bleeding spastic, she's in the room.' And they all stood up and I said, 'Excuse me, what was that you just said', and he said, 'Oh, nothing, Miss' and I said, 'Well, what did you just call him?', and he said, 'Oh, a spastic, Miss', and I said, 'What does that mean to

Changing for the 21st Century

you?' 'Oh, he's thick, he's dim, he's mental', and I said, 'Well, let me tell you one thing, he's not a spastic, but I am', and this boy had to sit down, he was so shocked, and his eyes came bulging out, and he said, 'But you can't be Miss, you're teaching us.'

"I said, 'Well this is your lucky day, Owen. You're being taught by a full-blown spastic', and we got talking about it in a way that I'd never talked about it before. I found out in that lesson that there were various kids in the class – one whose uncle had a special car that he drove around, because... another whose mother had an artificial limb, because... And they came out with all their things, and it was a marvellous talking point,

'Spastics News' was re-named 'Disability Now'

Changing Society

and nowadays of course they don't use it any more, so you haven't got that opening gambit: cerebral palsy just covers a multitude of sins somehow. I don't know, it's just too correct for me: I want my golliwog back. I like my golliwog."

These views are not unique. I remember very clearly that while I was in the PR department at the time when *Spastics News* became *Disability Now*, there was a lot of mail protesting about the change with people writing along the lines of "How dare you, I'm a spastic and I'm proud of it." There is a tendency to assume that such viewpoints are from an older generation. Rosamund is younger than I am. Make of that what you will.

The others I interviewed were a little less critical than she was about the name, though some had reservations. This is what they said:

William Burn: *"I can understand the reason for it, but I think we lost a lot of goodwill, especially with the older generation of people: not just spastics, but the people who raise money and so on. It cost us a lot. There were people who've said to me quite often in the last few years 'Why should we contribute to Scope when they spend all that money in having to paint all these different names on vans and publicity, and new letterheads for this and that?' They shuddered at the thought, because occasionally this information came out.*

"I think that we've had a setback because of the change of name. Now it can still prove the right thing to have done in years to come, but it's cost us money and time, in our growth, and in the public support for us. I say this quite objectively. I would have preferred another name, because if you're to have a short name, it should be the initials of what the short word is for, but s.c.o.p.e, apart from having the letters 'cp' for cerebral palsy and 's' for spastic... people do say 'What does this mean?'

"Fortunately, Anthony Hewson was here when we discussed

this, and I wasn't going to vote against him like that; I'm not that short-sighted, but I did say to Anthony, 'Please, if you're going to do this, it's important to say what we mean', and that's why you've got this little logo now, 'Scope, for people with cerebral palsy'. That helps people to understand what it's about, otherwise they do flounder about the name and wonder what on earth it means."

Alex Moira: *"There should be a new name, definitely, because I think that 'spastic' has become a sort of dirty word, or downgraded word, and something had to be done to get rid of that. Whether 'Scope' was the right answer or not, I don't know.*

"I was still connected with Llanlivery [the activity centre Churchtown Farm] while that discussion was raging, and I used to meet the then Chairman occasionally, at meetings, and talk with him, but I didn't feel that I had any contribution to make."

Tim Yeo: *"On the specific question of the name, I did have – though it's not for me to say, because I'm not part of it – I had strong reservations about the name change, because I don't think 'Scope' makes it very clear to the outsider what it's all about. Here was an organisation, which did have quite a powerful brand image. Well, you may want to change the brand image, but I think you need to show that it's still working in the disability field and 'Scope' doesn't necessarily explain that clearly. It would not have been a name that I would have chosen myself: but nevertheless it's been chosen and it's achieving recognition now."*

This chapter brings the identity of Scope almost up to date. With the name change the organisation faced the 21st century. I asked everyone to assess Scope as it is today. This is what they told me:

Andrew Berry: *"We've got rid of a lot of our large institutions, whereas when I joined, the majority of the services were fairly institutionalised. I'm very happy to have got rid of all those.*

Changing Society

"We've moved a long way. I'm not claiming responsibility for that: I've just been a part of the process, which has moved us from where we were 14 years ago to where we are now, but I am reasonably happy.

"For an organisation of its size, Scope punches a hell of a big punch within the social services world. You have to remember that our turnover is 0.1% of the social services provided by the Government. I think, in terms of our influence, it's much greater than 0.1%. We could of course always do better, but considering the unfashionableness of the disability issues at the moment, I don't think we do a bad job."

Rosamund Browne: "I think somebody somewhere will always need something like Scope. The only time we hear anything from Scope is not when anything good happens, but when something bad happens and Scope has stepped in to say something about it, and I think, in an ideal world we shouldn't need these charities anyway, but that's Utopian, isn't it? It's a pity that we need any of these charities, really, but I think all the needs from people really ought to be government-funded."

William Burn: "I think it's carried on doing most of the right things: becoming better known in the country as a leading charity, and it's continued the policy, which I particularly commend, of integration in schools and other things like that, in life as a whole, for disabled people."

Sir John Cox: "There's such a change, even from ten years ago, in encouraging and making possible persons to live at home, to not be institutionalised: for young people to be able to go mainstream in education as much as possible. I think it needs a great deal of financial help to allow Scope to have the objectives that it has today. I'm full of admiration for the new trend to de-institutionalise persons who should never have been institutionalised in the first place."

Hilda Davies: *"I don't know how many cerebral palsied people are working for it. I find attitudes still in Scope, like everywhere I suppose, how we know what's good for you – and they dish it out accordingly. In my fairly recent experience parents today want mainly social integration. The fighting spirit of 50 years ago seems to have been diluted and replaced by the 'rights' attitude which seems to dismiss experience and, as far as I can see, Scope and their conferences are full of able-bodied people. Where are these cerebral palsied people? In my opinion Scope is not fulfilling its full duty."*

Pat Entwhistle: *"I think they're making progress. They're getting more people with cerebral palsy interested in the running of Scope. But, at the end of the day, I still worry how far they're going to allow people with cerebral palsy to have the power: whether they'll just go so far, and that's it.*

"Scope is supposed to be one of the leading organisations which is providing services for local authorities. I personally have yet to see where this is being done: regarding education, respite, etc."

Bill Hargreaves: *"It's become too centralised. They have forgotten that their core work is for children, adults and parents who are dealing with cerebral palsy. They've been driven along by the fact that many people have joined without understanding what cerebral palsy really is all about; about the multiplicity of disabilities in one body that a person can have; about the difficulties of living in society; about the difficulties of finding work; the myriad of problems that face a person; their parents and friends; how to help him or her to achieve a realistic life, bearing in mind some quite appalling difficulties."*

Anthony Hewson: *"I think Scope is now seen by the public as a more relevant organisation to the people it serves. I'm not sure whether or not people really know what Scope is for and about. I'm not sure whether people know what cerebral palsy is.*

"Its aims should be, primarily, to represent the interests and needs of people with cerebral palsy. It would do that best by firstly developing new structures where people with cerebral palsy are properly represented at all levels throughout the whole organisation. That does mean imposing certain limits, as we did in the Partnership Committees. It was interesting that although the Council imposed limits, they didn't need to, because the moment people felt we were more relevant, they came themselves. Nobody ever needed to impose a limit on the Council, it just happened. That's the way it should be, and there should be a lot more of that.

"It should only run services of excellence – pioneering and developing services, educational services, residential services. It should not be involved in the day-to-day delivery of what is essentially a government responsibility. It should be running the very best, simply so it can say – and you have to run them to say it – 'We do this, we know what it costs.' We do have the qualifications to say, 'We understand this', and then we should parcel it up and say 'Get on with it.'"

John Queenborough: "As an organisation for a client, they never let anything slip regarding your welfare. If I have a fall, I just have to ring down, like yesterday and they come up. You are treated like a first-class citizen, which I am. It's very nice. I think Scope is a fine organisation. It is renowned throughout the world."

Glynn Vernon: "We've a lot of changes in the structure of Scope. Some of these changes could only work if people get involved. If people go on saying... 'Scope hasn't changed, therefore I won't join', then Scope won't change. But what is there now is that the infrastructure allows people to become involved and change things. That wasn't there before. The only members of Scope were the local groups... People who had got the best *possible motives, and who were really important in the early days. Maybe people like you and me, or younger people than we are, ought to be involved now. Now it's possible, but it wasn't possible before.*

"*I have noticed in the last year, that disabled people are becoming involved in the partnership areas, and they weren't really involved in the old regional structure. Even people from the BCODP [British Council Of Disabled People] are now becoming involved. We have a relationship now, with the BCODP, (well, they might not like to admit it openly, but it is there).*

"*I think Scope at the moment is in transition. I think it's looking for a future. It's still tied up a lot in the past. It's still got a lot of services, which it didn't know how to get rid of, because people are still using them, and a lot of people don't know any other alternative, and Scope feels that it owes those people something – which it does. But I'm not sure that the answer is to carry on in the way that they were.*"

Tim Yeo: "*I think that Scope does have a very creditable role now: a campaigning role. When I was Chairman of the [Conservative Party] Disability Group about two years ago, I was encouraged by the extent to which we were getting clear recommendations from Scope on a number of things, particularly the Disability Discrimination legislation, because the House was considering it at that time. I was encouraged to think that Scope was continuing what I think had been a very honourable tradition of trying to influence public policy, and I think that it's been successful at doing that. I'm not sure, because of the rather special relationship I've had with the organisation, whether I'm the most dispassionate judge of its success as a campaigner, because that was so dear to my heart when I was actually in charge of the organisation.*

"*I think today there is an even bigger role for a large voluntary organisation like Scope than there was 20 or 30 years ago. I think that people have got used to seeing voluntary organisations providing services and getting paid for them by the State. I think that's become an accepted structure and I think it's a good structure. I think that people have got used to voluntary organisations having a strong cutting edge in campaigning terms, which, 20 years ago, was a bit of a radical idea. There was some suggestion that charitable organisations might be breaking the law if they did too much campaigning, because they're not supposed to get involved in any kind of party political activity. I think those fears are much less great today: so I think that it has a big role there too.*

"I think that there's a better, but not an adequate, understanding of the potential role for disabled people to play in running any organisation, but particularly a voluntary organisation working in this field. I think that Scope's success in the last 20 years in helping to change attitudes towards disability should be a spur to continuing that, because there's so much more to be done. I think the fact that some success has been achieved. That should be an encouragement to work even harder at it."

In the context of the nineties, the success that Tim refers to is mainly to the credit of Anthony Hewson. His other main claim to fame, apart from the making the organisation more democratic and representative of people with cerebral palsy (and of course making a decisive move concerning the name), was to finally eliminate the public perception that Scope was against Conductive Education, the system of learning developed in Hungary for children with movement difficulties. The BBC fuelled the controversy with two documentaries about a young British boy who was being taken to the Pető Institute in Budapest, allegedly because the treatment was unavailable in

Britain. The impression was that Scope did not want to know about the apparently revolutionary form of therapy. In actual fact the very school that Anthony's son, Toby attended, had been involved in Conductive Education for some time before the row. As he was already involved with Ingfield Manor School through Toby, Anthony took up the issue as Chairman of Scope.

Now looking back, how does he see Scope?

"It has been an interesting experience and it's demonstrated to me that there are serious limitations to what an organisation the size of Scope, with its paymasters, can achieve, and I hadn't realised that when I was there. In fact I think I led myself into believing it could change the world. This was a most serious error of judgement.

"I think the reason is very straightforward: I think that big organisations always have to remember they're in the public eye, they're getting large amounts of government money: Scope gets, whether anybody likes it or not, £25 million to £30 million out of its turnover of £90m from local government. I am convinced the big charities have modified their stance on a whole range of issues, not for any conspiratorial reason or whatever but to keep the money coming.

"I have very little to do with Scope anymore. But I get the newsletters and I'm an honorary life member, so I receive these things, and now I'm reading about budgets being cut again, shortage of money because the rag trade's gone into recession... I recognise all the language. It's like deja vu.

"They're still doing work on the Vision and things, and my hope is that that will come through now, but they have to get away from this inward-looking thing."

In one way, at least, Anthony is, in my opinion, unique. Although he is, of course, a parent first and foremost, he was able to look beyond that and see the perspective of someone

Changing Society

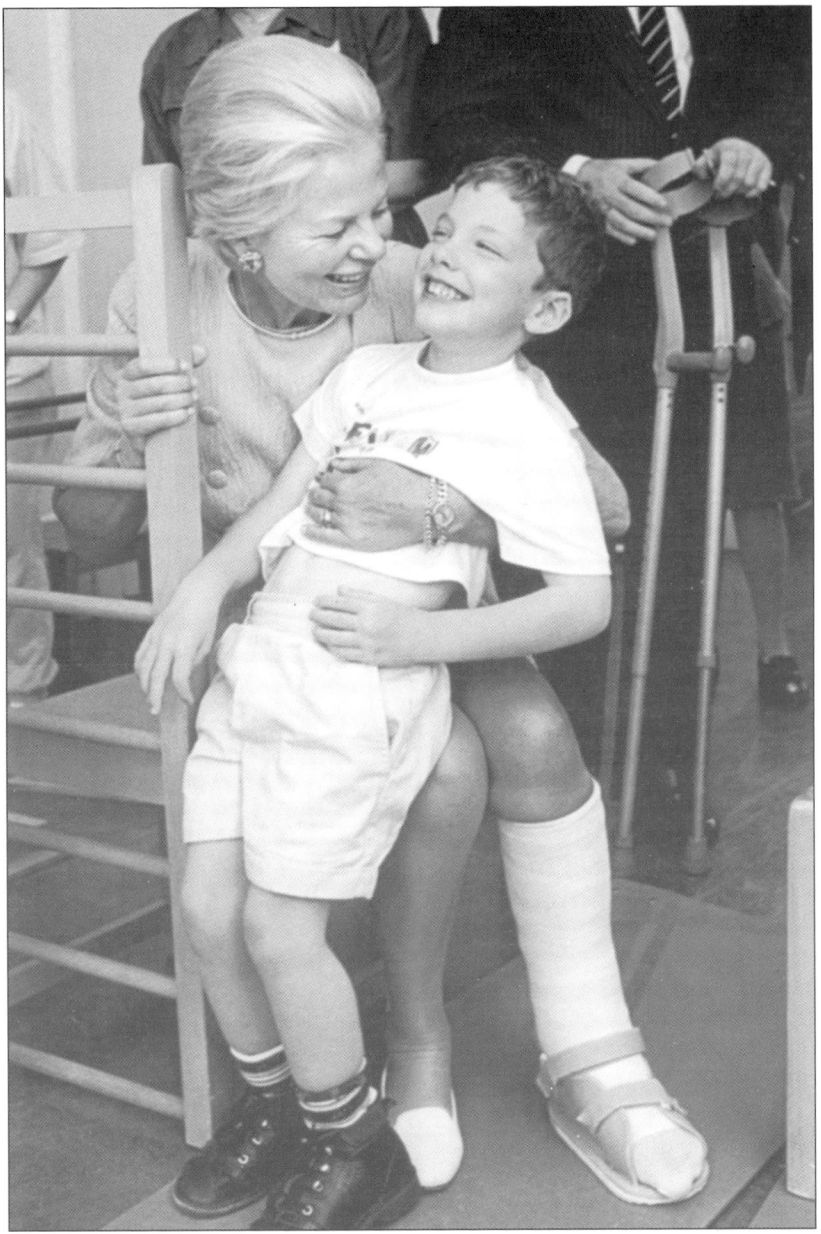

The Duchess of Kent visits Pető UK in 1992　　　PHOTO: MAGGIE MURRAY

with cerebral palsy. I asked him about the potential conflict between being a parent speaking on behalf of someone with cerebral palsy and trying to give a voice to people with cerebral palsy.

"I didn't ever find it difficult to reconcile the parent/person with the disability issue. I found that if I listened properly, there was very little difference in where we were coming from. Glynn and I had some very sharp conversations – and we still do – about the issues around euthanasia and genetics: Glynn and I started a long way apart on that. I remember there was one meeting when Glynn said 'I'd tell the whole lot to ****ing well go home' and I said, 'If I could prevent another child being born with cerebral palsy, that's what I'd do.' So we were at opposite ends of the world. We've talked about it a lot, very privately, often, and with a fair amount of booze inside us on one occasion – Johnny Walker does help sometimes – and having talked it through a lot, our views are not really very far apart. I think that's been a growing process. He undoubtedly taught me about the value of life, no matter what your 'difference' is to so-called 'normal' people..."

Whilst Anthony was Chairman, his Vice Chair was Glynn Vernon. For some time he stayed away from Scope but he returned hoping he could change the organisation for the better. Glynn will be the first to acknowledge the support and the friendship of Anthony Hewson.

I asked Anthony what impact Scope had had on him:

"Scope changed my life. I think it's changed my life because it's changed my values. Before Toby was born and I understood what it meant to be the parent of a young person with disability, (I'll never understand what it's like to have a disability because I haven't got one)... the biggest single impact I suppose it's made is in the understanding of what society does to people *who are at, by dint of birth, the bottom of the heap and it's appalling. I don't believe most of it's done deliberately; I think some of it's done deliberately. The most extraordinary irony from where I stand is that I think most of it is done with good intention, but the results are, bluntly, a sodding catastrophe. I mean the overall result, starting with the intent to assist, is nearly always a sodding catastrophe of immense proportions. What it says to me is governments should not fiddle around with individuals' lives. They've got no idea how to do it. They always make a cock-up of it. They should leave it to the organisation and to the people themselves...*

"My perception changed over the years because of people like you, to start with! There are some very special people, who've become friends now, who've had a very profound influence on me. I mean people like Valerie Lang and Glynn: those people who've actually been at the forefront of trying to change things.

"I had some very difficult times to start with. A lot of this is emotional; it's ridiculous to deny it. I think the harsh bit was at the beginning, because people would say things to me which, for quite a raw parent, were quite difficult to put my mind round.

"I think the first two or three years as Chairman was a very testing period. It was very difficult sometimes. Bluntly, as you well know, Chris, people like Valerie and Glynn brook no quarter when it comes to this sort of issue. You don't get let off any hooks: you get on and do it and defend your patch."

For me the decade was a mixture of experiences. Since the early 1980s I was living independently in London and after working in the PR department of Scope I moved onto freelance work. At the beginning of the 1990s I was one of three presenters on the BBC2 disability programme *One in Four*. I was also in the middle of a long spell as TV critic of *Disability Now*. To my complete amazement I was awarded the OBE in this decade. In 1999 I was elected Chairman of the Executive Working Group of the Scope London Partnership Committee. I also tried, and failed (twice), to be elected to the Executive Council.

2000 and Beyond

Changing Society

Alan Martin and fellow speaker Paul Boateng MP at a conference in 1998

2000 and Beyond

In November 1996, the Scope AGM voted in favour of an individual membership scheme to give a voice to the 25,000 people that Scope and its local groups are in contact with every year.

How do the new members view the organisation?

Alan Martin lives independently in the Merseyside area and is a founder member of the North West Partnership Committee. He attends many conferences, making addresses through his Liberator speech synthesiser. He describes his association with Scope like this:

"I became involved with Scope about three years ago in 1996 personally, but before that I had heard of Scope because my family had applied to them for a grant. I also heard of them when my friend applied to try and buy his Liberator. I was 33 when I first became involved.

"I've been actively involved for over two years, since Rod [Scope's community fieldworker] came to visit me and asked me to help in raising awareness about difficulty of getting patient aids, by becoming a member of the CALL [Communication Aid

Lending Library] committee, which is supported by Scope. He also asked if I'd be interested in serving on the local transition committee. I said yes, and since then have been actively involved with the local Partnership Committee, I attend all the Executive Committee meetings and consider and monitor grant applications. I attend local and national annual general meetings. I would like to be on the Executive Committee of Scope sometime in the future. As well as work I have done on Scope, Scope has helped me a great deal. When I began to set up my own home, 18 months ago, Scope gave me small grants to help furnish my home. Also a student social worker, who was on a placement with Liverpool Scope, came and helped me with all kinds of practical things. The Partnership Committee supports me, too. They have provided me with computer equipment to enable me to do the work."

Like most of us he is not uncritical of the organisation.

"I think that perhaps Scope was not considering the wishes of the individual with cerebral palsy, but rather working for the needs of the family, also perhaps following the medical model of disability, I'm talking about perhaps ten years ago.

"I think that Scope doesn't address the needs of older people with cerebral palsy, people about my own age and older than myself, as much as they should be."

If you think that that is strong criticism, that's nothing compared to the views of Alison John and Angela Smith. Alison has been the subject of a number of BBC documentaries since 1981, including one centred on her marriage. These were about her early life. It was afterwards that things changed for her.

"Later in adulthood, I became a consultant in disabilities and an equality trainer. That was in 1990. Through the BBC and Scope asking me to try things out and give my opinion on different

things, as a professional. They buy in my services on a freelance basis either as a consultant or as a trainer. I get asked at different levels to work with Scope, with different partnerships, with different development projects, which are around."

Through this work she has formed a not very complimentary opinion of the organisation:

"As far I'm concerned, Scope are still very disabling, they don't practise what they preach, as far as inclusion and rights and it's not about inclusion and rights. Staff are still very much working from the medical perception of what this disability is, they aren't aware that it is now a social issue rather than a medical issue. Disabled people within Scope have said they are very disempowered, very much passive in their roles, aren't able to really have their needs met. I think Scope are still working from a charity model, and not a model which is about empowering and about change. So I think the question is really, who is Scope there for? Them or for us?

"But there are pockets of good practice. I have done some work recently in the East Midlands region, they are willing to listen and accept how practice really should be, they are really actually listening to people with cerebral palsy. Fifteen – twenty years ago that wouldn't have happened.

"One of the dilemmas in Scope is who is it they are for? If they could get their heads around that and make a firm decision that would stop a lot of the difficulties they are having. Some of the people I know with cerebral palsy want to be in power and included, but the parents and others say, 'Hold on, we don't know.' So, there are pockets of positive things happening.

"It is beginning to recognise that it needs to promote inclusion rather than segregation, and certainly the Scope skill centres have been under a hell of a lot of fire, from people like myself who believe in inclusion. I think that it is interesting. In Scope's

Changing Society

aim they say we promote inclusion and then on the other hand it runs these segregating schools. So it is a very mixed message about what it is trying to promote.

"In my opinion, Scope today is lost. I think they're trying to be something they're not. On one hand they talk about inclusion, rights and equality and yet on the other hand they have what I call day wasting centres, where people just go and waste. There's no equality in that. But I think they're confused, I also think they've also got a problem because they are a charity, they need to raise money, if they seem to be too rights-orientated they won't raise enough dosh."

Apart from the fact they are both critical of Scope, there are other common factors between Alison John and Angela Smith. Both are only connected with Scope through their work. In Angela's own words:

"I am not a member. I'm only involved through my current work, as a Young Disabled People's Outreach Worker for Brent Association of Disabled People. Scope funded the project with Brent and Harrow Health Authority."

And this is what she thinks of the organisation: *"What I remember is that it was very much controlled by non-disabled people, and professionals, more or less dictating how people with cerebral palsy should live their lives, and it didn't seem like they listened much to what we wanted. I remember feeling very bad about the name 'Spastics Society'. I think it gave me a bad feeling about cerebral palsy, because the word 'spastic' took on a very negative...You know, it became a kind of abuse: a word you use when you want to put somebody down... I think that affected how I felt about having cerebral palsy, and when I was younger, I used to say 'If I had to be disabled, I wish I had a different impairment', because I was impaired by spinal injury, it seemed to upset more than to have cerebral palsy: I blame that on the organisation, Scope, because they perpetuated that by keeping the old name for so long, that I feel they have to acknowledge that they played a big part in creating the low self-esteem somebody had to live with.*

"There are some changes. There are more disabled people in it. Scope has also been doing a lot more campaigning on disability rights, but the thing is, they still have non-disabled people in the powerful positions. I feel they're more like government lackeys. I think they work more with the government than they do with the grass roots disabled people. It needs to be more democratic. It's not.

"It's definitely better than 'The Spastics Society': I'm not against it, but it doesn't really say much. I know what 'scope' means, but they should have picked a name that gave an insight into what it's doing for people with cerebral palsy: they could have chosen a more in-your-face name.

"I do think it needs to be more disability civil rights-orientated, but I do acknowledge that Scope does do useful work, specifically of benefit towards cerebral palsy, that might not be relevant to other impairment groups. One example... Conductive Education: it does benefit some people, and that wouldn't be relevant to other impairment groups. But on the whole, I think it is doing more for all disabilities in the organisation, but should still keep a part of it where it is specific to the needs of people with cerebral palsy."

In the 1990s Ian Dawson-Shepherd died. Bill Hargreaves wrote his obituary. Some of the words Bill used could equally fit him.

"Ian Dawson-Shepherd was perhaps the greatest campaigner and friend of cerebral palsied people and their parents. Thanks to the work of The Spastics Society, which he founded in 1952, the attitudes towards cerebral palsy have changed dramatically, so while before the 1950s it was rare even to see a person with

Changing Society

Toby Hewson

cerebral palsy in public, they now have opportunities everywhere in society."

Oh, in case you thought I'd forgotten it's now time to introduce the second person whose association with Scope began in this decade. Actually, he is a major hope for the future. By the time Scope is 50 this man will be 20. He is Anthony Hewson's son Toby. His future and Scope's are intertwined.

Toby Hewson was born in the early 1980s. For much of his life he has been at Ingfield Manor School. During all that time, Anthony and Elizabeth, his parents, have been involved with the organisation. Only comparatively recently has Toby himself chosen to be involved. To those who know Scope well, he has already a reputation for championing the cause of youth membership. Scope has to meet the needs of people of Toby's age, if it is to remain relevant in the 21st century. Here are Toby's views of Scope today and in the future:

"Scope should be fighting for disabled people's rights. Providing support for all disabled people, not just those newly diagnosed. I think that the organisation should be primarily focusing on people with cerebral palsy, but also including all forms of disability. If Scope does exist in the future, hopefully it will have a disabled person as chairman... A chairman with a disability will have to be twice as good as any able-bodied chairman Scope has known.

"Scope needs to do a lot more campaigning, to try to change the attitudes of the world. Basically, Scope needs to change, so it is benefiting the people who really need it. Us, the disabled people."

In the 1950s disability was not on the political agenda. That's why individual charities were created to act in the interest of disabled people. Then, disability was seen as a set of physical or mental conditions. So, charities were impairment-based, as in the RNIB (for visually impaired people), RNID (for hearing impaired people). In this context, creating an organisation solely about cerebral palsy seemed logical and acceptable. But times change. Now disability is on the political agenda, but not in terms of different groups of disabled people. Political parties are more interested in the community of disabled people, than in particular sections of it.

It is against this background that there is a debate within the ranks of Scope. Should it remain an organisation only concerned with cerebral palsy, or should it be acting in the interest of all disabled people? These are the answers from my contributors.

Andrew Berry: *"I'm not sure how it's going to be significantly different in 10 years' time. There are a number of things we have to do that at the moment we aren't doing, but my overall impression, looking at how much can change in an organisation of Scope's complexity is that not very much will change. It takes*

Changing Society

Andrew Berry

a long time to alter things: not only that, but the services we deliver, whether you like it or not, people end up having their entire lives dominated by Scope, so you can't just pick up a policy and change it, no matter how you'd like to, because you've got to shake hands with the people you provide services for.

"I can see an opportunity for Scope to get more involved in more work. I can see threats for Scope: in particular, issues like the National Lottery, which seem to be undermining our independence, to a large extent. I've been in Council meetings where we've said, 'Oh we can't do that, because the National Lottery won't fund us.' Now that to me is a huge worry, because one of the major things about Scope is our independence, and I'd hate us to lose that: I'd hate us to be more controlled than we are at the moment.

"For example, the reason why we're having this debate at the moment about whether Scope is for people with cerebral palsy or more generally for people with disabilities – one of the main drives for us to have that debate is that we're being forced into it by local authorities, who are saying that they will not provide funding for single disability organisations. I think when an organisation gets that controlled by its funders, then perhaps the current thinking that certain funding should lose their charitable status will grow in voice, with a populist government like we've got at the moment.

"Look, I'm old enough to remember why Scope was founded initially, and the reason was because people with cerebral palsy did not have a loud enough voice among the competing disabled groups. If you want me to tell you what I think about the issue of disability versus cerebral palsy, I will. I'm 100 per cent behind the idea that Scope has to retain its identity as an organisation of, for, whatever you call it, people with cerebral palsy, and the reason for that is that I still feel at the bottom of the pile. I still feel that other disabilities have more influence than I would without Scope."

William Burn: *"We were, by our Memorandum and Articles of Association, incorporated to help people with cerebral palsy, and that's what we've done: but, wherever possible, even in my day, we gave positive thinking to helping other disabled charities or people, if it was going to help us mutually. Take the Paediatric Research Unit: we spent a lot of money, setting up a Chair in Guy's Hospital. £400,000, when we first started putting it up for one Chair, which had to be funded: then more after that. There were probably lots of people who thought 'Well, why can't all this be spent on spastics?' but we were finding out the cause of spasticity: but in that, 99 times out of 100 you find other reasons for people being born disabled, or dying* *prematurely or so on. But you have to help other charities in trying to help yourself. Providing there's a mutual interest, I'm all for helping wherever you can."*

Sir John Cox: "*If you're asking me to stick my neck out and say 'Should it be pan-disability?', the answer is 'No'. I don't believe that. That would be an absolute hotchpotch. I don't see the advantage of making it 'pan'. Cerebral palsy is so individual, so particular, that I feel that one should stay with cerebral palsy: and more than that, I can't tell you: research, and continue the good work."*

Hilda Davies: "*I don't think it fits very well in today's world. It hasn't enough teeth. It doesn't make the general public aware of the problems of cerebral palsy. I just don't think they realised how people with cerebral palsy have to cope with it, especially those with good brains, who want to be independent. I think that they need and want to work and a lot of them, have qualifications that should make them be a great help to those who are providing for cerebral palsied people – they know what it's like – why does Scope think it knows what it's like, when it's full, so far as I can see, of able-bodied people?... How many are there who are working for Scope? That's the way Scope is not fitting into the world of today."*

Anthony Hewson: "*I think people will only join if they feel the organisation is going in a progressive direction, and the more momentum you pick up, the more people will join in with it. I think its primary focus must remain on cerebral palsy. I think if it leaves that, there will be immense problems, but that does not mean to say that it will not. It must represent the wider needs of people with disability a lot of the time."*

Valerie Lang: "*I would say further that I hope Scope does not move towards a body entirely of disabled people, because I see, certainly in the early years, I see parents as being clients, almost*

2000 and Beyond

Valerie Lang

equally with their small children, and possibly again, in old age. I think this is one fact that makes Scope unique among disability charities, in that, at some stages of the life of a disabled person, their family are almost as much clients of Scope as the disabled person is, and, for that reason, I think parents should never be pushed entirely off its committee structure. I think they have a right to be there. I don't think they have a right to a majority, but they have a right, in my opinion, to a significant voice.

"*I believe that Scope's first loyalty must be to the needs of people with cerebral palsy, and if people with other disabilities can benefit from this work, then I'm happy to let them benefit, but I do think the first loyalty must remain with the needs of people with cerebral palsy.*"

Alan Martin: "*It should be primarily for people with cerebral palsy but not excluding people with other disabilities.*"

John Queenborough: "*I think it should be all round. I think if it embraces all the smaller organisations, other disabled people are welcome so they won't have to fight for funding for their* *own. I think it's good to bring other people with other disabilities in to the realm of Scope."*

Glynn Vernon: *"I think that, apart from Radar... there isn't a national organisation which represents the interests of disabled people. A lot of what we do has to involve all disabled people. We're not in the real world if we try to define disabled people by impairments. If we say we believe in the social model – and we do, don't we? – how can we turn round and say we want to represent people with a medical condition, and we don't care about anybody else?*

"I want Scope to be a disability organisation. I'm quite happy for it to have a special expertise in cerebral palsy. I recognize there are unique problems which people with cerebral palsy might have, which they may need special support with. I'm quite happy for Scope to do that, but to say, 'That's all we do...'"

Tim Yeo: *"I think that cerebral palsy is a sufficiently large client group: it's a sufficiently large subject, to be worthy of an entirely specialist organisation, but it's also clearly the case that many of the issues which affect cerebral palsied people also affect people with other disabilities, and you don't want to waste a resource by confining the aim too narrowly: and this applies, I think both to services and to campaigning. Again, just to illustrate it from my own time: one of the successful campaigns we ran was not on a policy issue at all, but it was to keep open Tadworth Court, which at that time was the country branch of Great Ormond Street Hospital. Great Ormond Street wanted to close this in 1982 and we linked up with other organisations whose own client group used the services at Tadworth Court, and it was only by having a joint approach that we were able to succeed."*

This debate will run and run. How it is resolved will shape the future of Scope. What is this future? What is Scope like at the

2000 and Beyond

beginning of the 21st Century? I asked everyone I interviewed about these questions and also about how Scope impacted on them as individuals and on society generally. Here are their answers:

Andrew Berry: *"I would say that the last 40 or 50 years have seen a recognition that a whole lot of groups of people who were at one time marginalised from society have a contribution to make to society, and I think Scope... packs a bigger punch than its size implies. It's difficult to identify any particular aspect; it's just been part of a general society-wide movement."*

Rosamund Browne: *"Undoubtedly it had a tremendous impact, in that it gave me many opportunities which ordinary 'normal' society didn't offer me, or weren't prepared to offer me, didn't want to offer me; didn't think it was possible to offer me. They were brave enough to set up a school that offered the same opportunities to you and to me...*

"It was a tremendously courageous step, to set up a school such as Delarue, to make it a grammar school, and to make the expectations high. You weren't just going to leave school and do work behind a desk or in a sheltered workshop...You were expected to go on to further..."

Hilda Davies: *"Will there ever be a disabled person as Chief Executive? Oh yes, providing they can do it and they have enough help to do it. Why shouldn't they? I can't really understand this question at all. If they've got the brains and the mind to do it. If they need help, they should be given it. So far as I'm concerned more emphasis on the severely disabled who need physical help to do the work is what is necessary and I don't think they are doing that right now."*

Bill Hargreaves: *"Today, Scope is a tremendous amalgam of work being done for people with disabilities, who perhaps have lost their way, because they find it difficult to understand the* *antecedents of the organisation: the raison d'être for it. They need to look very closely, I think, at what they're doing…*

"*I think that everything they do needs a fresh look at why they're doing it and how valid it is for the you's and me's of cerebral palsy life…*

"*That's where a large organisation can lose its way and I think that that is the danger: that it is losing its way. It has lost its way, largely. It's found a lot of good ways. It's forged ahead in many excellent ways, but in other ways, it's sadly fallen down. When I have to cope with people wanting help from our tiny charity [Handicapped Aid Trust] because they can't go to Scope, because Scope can't help them, there's something wrong somewhere. Scope ought to be able to help them and Scope ought to look at what it's doing. Why can't this person have a holiday? Why can't we find the money for him? What are we spending on other things that we could stop and spend here?*"

Anthony Hewson: "*I think during its first 20 years or so, it had a very profound impact on society and then I think it stopped. How old is it now? Nearly 50? I would have said that for its first 20 years it had a very profound impact: for the next 20 it stood still. It probably allowed the public to get off the hook a bit. It may have been a combination of things: people may not have been ready to take much more: all sorts of things came into play – you have to look at the full context that organisations are working in. It could not have carried on at the rate it was, it was just impossible. It certainly did stand still. It may well have gone backwards. I think in the last two or three years, it's created another opportunity from which it can move forward again. It can be part of the leadership of the movement. It should not try to do that alone. It should be part of an overall process at work, but I think it has created an opportunity now where it can, if it moves positively, and in an* *organised and systematic way, and if it supports organisations that can say and do things that it can't do: if it buries some of its arrogance, because it is a terribly arrogant organisation – but I think it needs to learn to work with others a lot more, to maximise the opportunities it's created."*

"I suspect for Toby the real influence of Scope on me is that I hope he feels that he's grown up with a positive view of disability. I hope he hasn't grown up with a lot of the baggage that I know a lot of the people like Valerie and Glynn had to endure, and indeed still endure to some degree.

"I mean, he's very fortunate in terms of generations. He's arrived in a generation where the level of discrimination is substantially lower than at probably any time in the history of our nation. I suspect he's probably got better opportunities now, Chris, than at any previous time. Maybe we've got to do a bit of work on employment together, to really sort that out.

"What I'd like to feel now is that he becomes part of that push – not with me, I mean on his own."

Valerie Lang: *"I think it has been a large impact, whether or not the average person knows what Scope is, or what The Spastics Society was. I think the Society gave a name to the condition: OK, it trained people to call us 'spastics', and I know that became a term of abuse, but before The Spastics Society existed, there were people with cerebral palsy, who apparently hardly knew why they were as they were, and I know that generation was much more comfortable, once it had a name to put to the condition, and an explanation for why they looked and acted the way they did. The Society, and now Scope, has educated the public. It has, together with other organisations, brought disability much more onto the national agenda. I think it helped, through its schools: it probably paved the way for education. It pioneered a lot of the community resources,* certainly the community living. I think it's had a huge impact and I am proud of it."

Alan Martin: "Most people have only heard about Scope's charity shops and not about the work that Scope does. Charity shops should publicise Scope's campaigns and aims, as well as just thinking about fundraising. They provide a good opportunity for disability awareness raising and could reach a large part of the general public.

"I'd like to see a future world where Scope was not needed, I'd like to see Scope just leading and ensuring that all disabled people got the services they are entitled to from the Government. Not needing to fight and campaign for a thing, which are so obviously people's entitlements as their human right in a civilised society. I'd like to see Scope pushing forward the DDA, to have some real teeth and be the sword of legislation which disabled people work forward and design for themselves."

Alex Moira: "I think, in the early years, it was a model of a modern, efficient charity, that had a way of touching the public's heart, which many other organisations envied, and quite a number of them cried 'Foul!', and I think in the later times, its concern with the medical aspects, and its patronage of medicine, has again been very important. Some of the long-term commitments it took on were really surprising for a charity."

John Queenborough: "I would like to think that probably the number of cerebral palsy people will be fewer, because of improved treatments and even a cure. I would say that within 20 years, the number of cerebral palsy people will be greatly diminished.

"Within my limitations, I have an opportunity to do things, by asking Scope to assist me in some way and they help. They have been my greatest support; knowing Scope would help me no matter what situation I am in.

2000 and Beyond

John Queenborough

"In 10 years' time, probably places like this [Scope's Princess Marina Centre in Buckinghamshire] will be closed. It will probably mean people will be in flats or apartments with a small skeletal staff to help them with things they can't do for themselves but I think it will be an ongoing thing. An organisation helping and carrying more people, helping to set people up in their own house. Helping people in their own environment." *(John has now moved to his own home in Woodford, Essex.)*

Angela Smith: *"I think apart from the last 10 years, I think they encouraged negative attitudes of us, being recipients of charity. I think they helped perpetuate that up until recently, and that isn't very helpful. But I think now they're doing more work on civil rights, I think their work now is more productive. I think they colluded with disablist attitudes, especially with those horrible dolls with the begging bowls and the callipers:*

Changing Society

I used to feel like kicking their heads in when I used to see those stupid dolls outside the shops.

"They need to send out a clear invitation to black people with cerebral palsy, to join Scope, because our contribution is just as valuable (as anyone else's), so that they can support the needs of the ethnic community. You can't expect black people just to come of their own accord: they don't perceive it as an organisation they should go to. They need to shout it out loud and clear."

Glynn Vernon: "Scope's impact on me has been immense. For a start, Scope educated me; well, The Spastics Society did anyway. It made me into the arrogant bastard I am. I have thought a lot about Delarue recently, and, philosophically, it goes against everything I believe: it is elitist, but it provided people with a damn good education, which I don't see now...

"Through our campaigns and PR work, I think we can and do affect attitudes in a pretty positive way, on the whole. We get it wrong sometimes, but since the early days, when we got it wrong all the time, we've come a long way. We've come a long way from 'Please help our spastics', so we've impacted a lot on attitudes, and we've affected Government policy, and I hope we've done that in a positive way as well.

"I think within 10 years we'll have a disabled Chair, and I think, after that, we'll never have an able-bodied Chair again. As for a disabled Chief Executive, that will come as well. I wouldn't like to put a time-scale on it, but it will come."

Glynn Vernon

2000 and Beyond

Tim Yeo: *"I'd like to think its future is to be at the forefront of innovation...*

"I would say that Scope's impact on society has been enormous. I think if you go right back to the beginning and think of the origins, which were a group of parents – and I have said some critical things about parents, but I don't want to be highly critical about them – who simply would not accept the conventional wisdom of the time, just after the War, which was that cerebrally palsied children were not capable of being educated in the same way that other children were, and they wouldn't take 'no' for an answer. It is enormously to their credit that they would not do so, because they altered attitudes to education by their single-mindedness...

"I think it's had a great impact, and I hope that your book is able to give that impression, because I think it's a record that few voluntary organisations could match: few could hardly come anywhere near it. In terms of what it's achieved, the impact that it's had and the way that attitudes have changed in the last 50 years, I think that Scope can claim a lot of credit for that, and I believe that should be recognised and I think that it would help the organisation to determine both what its role should be in the future and how that can be best achieved, if it has a good understanding of what's happened in the past."

Changing Society

Chris Davies

Conclusions

I hope very much that there will be a second volume to this history in 50 years' time. It may begin with Toby Hewson and Alan Martin. If Scope reinvents itself enough, the second volume may even feature Angela Smith, Alison John and Rosamund Browne as prominent active members! Stranger things have been known to happen.

Whether they like the organisation or not, there is no one in this book that would deny that Scope has had a significant role in their lives. Not even its severest critics would claim that Scope has done more harm than good. But it must be said that it has done some harmful things, even though the harm is only clear in retrospect.

Scope valued segregation for too long. Countless people have been isolated through education, accommodation and employment. It is easy to say that it would never happen today, and that at the time, it was acceptable. Actually, I would say it should never have been acceptable. Too many people have had their lives limited because of this, and no matter how much good the organisation has done, this is a wrong that should neither be ignored nor dismissed.

Scope is reforming itself. Independent living is now preferred to institutionalisation. Fewer children go to special school (though some would say not few enough). Open employment and not sheltered is the preferred option. However, the organisation still has much to do.

Earlier the contributors entered the debate concerning who Scope is about – people with cerebral palsy, or disabled people generally. In my opinion it should specialise in cerebral palsy, but not at the exclusion of concerns that are common to everyone in the disabled community. Goodness knows, there are enough of these! I would suggest, though that there is another debate that ought to be undertaken. This one is far more fundamental.

From its outset to the present day the driving force within Scope is that of parents. Even though there is now a majority of people with cerebral palsy on the Executive Council, there is no doubt that the influence of parents is still a dominant force in Scope. I have absolutely no doubt that this is where the organisation had to start. It could not have happened any other way. If people with cerebral palsy could have provided for themselves, Scope simply need not have been born. It was appropriate, necessary and right that parents originated the organisation.

But entities evolve. Simply because something starts one way, there is no reason why it should stay that way. The children that were the impetus for Scope's creation are now adults and part of a generation of disabled people who want to, and are able to, control their own lives. So the debate should be, should Scope be an organisation just for disabled people – mainly people with cerebral palsy – exclusively, or should it continue to be as much about parents as anyone else?

Conclusions

Parents of disabled people are notorious for not letting go. I will be the last person to say that this is easy. But if disabled people are increasingly considered equal in our society then part of that equality must include recognition of our capability and right to control our own affairs. I have no doubt that during this century it will happen. Let's hope this is soon.

Putting disabled people in charge of an organisation like Scope, even if they are the right people is, by no means, a 'magic wand' but it would be a wonderful signal that Scope actually believes in equality. Sir John Cox reminded me that once I had ambitions to be the first disabled Chief Executive of Scope. I did, but that was before I entered into management and found out for myself the harsh reality of this kind of responsibility. For a year, I was in charge of a small charity and I found the pressure truly awful. This was mainly because I had never had any experience like this before.

So it is no good expecting someone to survive in this kind of position without adequate preparation. Equally not many disabled people are fortunate enough to be given the opportunity to be managers. So although Scope, sooner or later, will have a disabled Chief Executive, it will happen sooner if the organisation offers training to winning candidates, which must also include mentoring by current members of staff. Because of my painful experience of management, I don't think that I will be applying. But the Chairmanship of Scope... that's a different matter entirely.

I have come to the end of my journey. It has been fascinating unravelling the threads. To guide me, I had two allies. Bill Elliott was asked to compile a history of Scope before I approached him. His text finished at the end of the 1970s, but it has nevertheless been invaluable. My other guide has been my project manager at Scope, Alex White. He has been constantly

Changing Society

supportive and his assistance and encouragement has been priceless.

Christy Brown wrote a book called *Down all the Days*. I wished he hadn't, because it was a damn good title. I have enjoyed going down all the days of Scope. I now appreciate the organisation much more than I did before I started. My thanks to the contributors for making the journey so interesting.

In each chapter of this book there have been key dates. The book itself has key dates. These are:

Spring 1998 – Scope commissioned this book
September 1998 – I began to write the text
December 1998 – I conducted my first interview
May 2000 – I conducted my final interview (the 17th)
December 2000 – I completed the text
May 2002 – the book is published.

These dates are here to show how much time has gone by already during the lifetime of this book, but, of course, the story will not end as you read the last page. Scope will go on and, perhaps even before this book is on the shelf, may have changed drastically since this text was finished. All I have been able to do is to tell the story through the experience of others. But the story has no end, at least not one that I can see. Hopefully, if there is an end it will be a positive one. Namely that Scope is no longer necessary.

Such a day would be on the last page of the next volume. It might be Utopia but then again, it might not be. Whether or not it happens Scope should be pleased with its first 50 years.

But, as the song says, "Things can only get better!"